Simpsons™ Comics
A-Go-Go

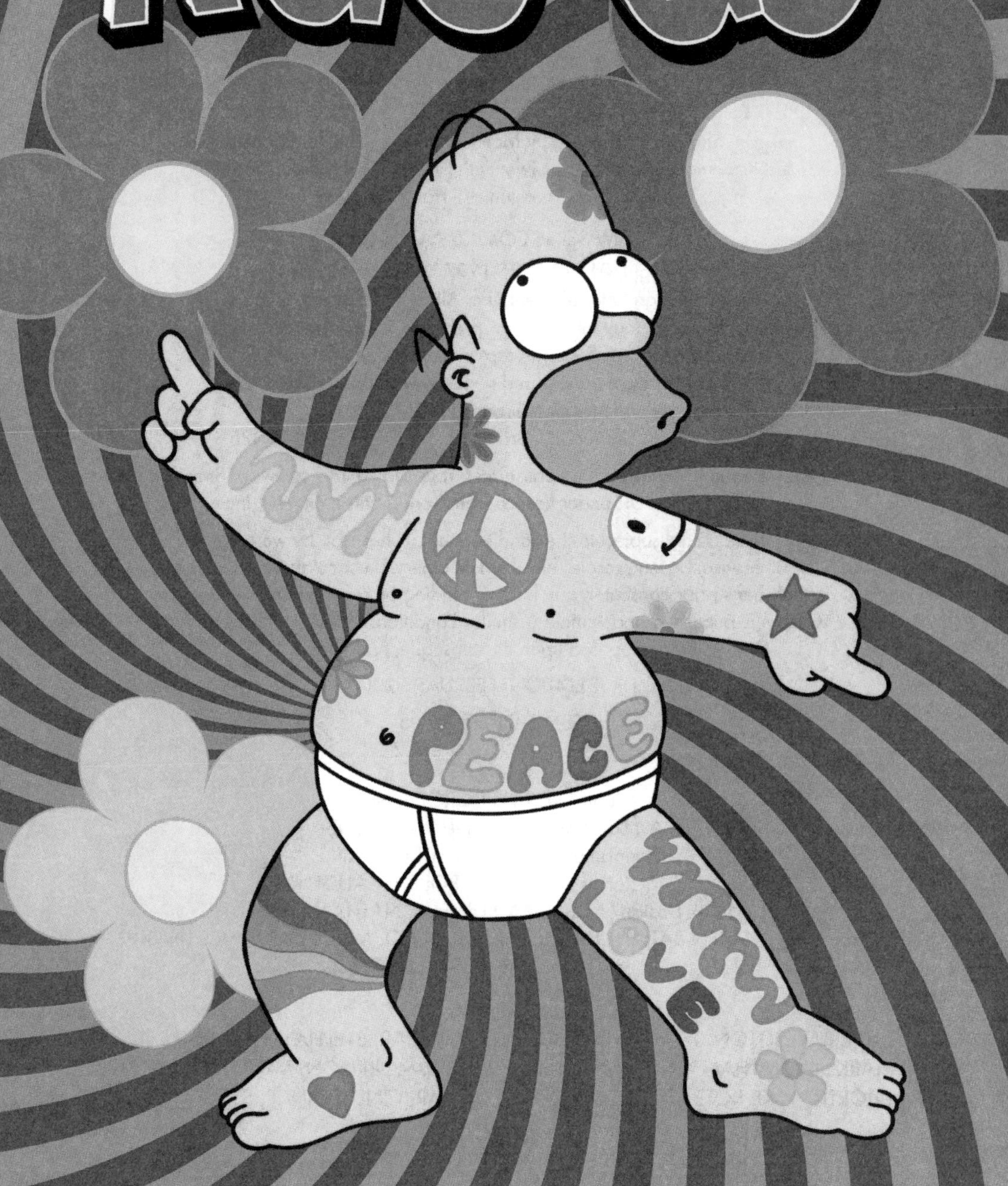
PEACE
LOVE

TITAN BOOKS

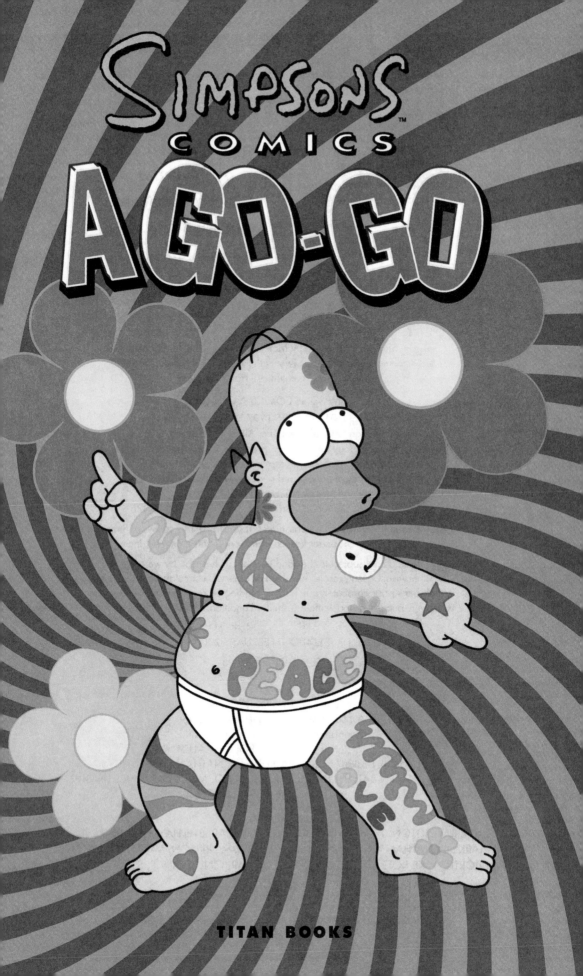

To the loving memory
of Snowball I:
Marge's abstract
art isn't the same
without you.

SIMPSONS COMICS A GO-GO

Copyright ©1992,1995,1997, 1998, & 1999 by
Bongo Entertainment, Inc. All rights reserved.
Bongo Comics Group c/o Titan Books
1440 S. Sepulveda Blvd., 3rd Floor, Los Angeles, CA 90025

Published in the UK by Titan Publishing Group Ltd., 144 Southwark Street,
London SE1 0UP, under licence from Bongo Entertainment, Inc.

FIRST EDITION: FEBRUARY 2000

ISBN 1-84023-151-3
1 3 5 7 9 10 8 6 4 2

Publisher: MATT GROENING
Art Director / Editor: BILL MORRISON
Managing Editor: TERRY DELEGEANE
Director of Operations: ROBERT ZAUGH
Book Design/Assistant Art Director: NATHAN KANE
Production: KAREN BATES, CHIA-HSIEN JASON HO, MIKE ROTE, CHRIS UNGAR
Legal Guardian: SUSAN GRODE

Contributing Artists:
TIM BAVINGTON, JEANNINE BLACK, LUIS ESCOBAR, STEPHANIE GLADDEN, TIM
HARKINS, NATHAN KANE, ROBERT KRAMER, BILL MORRISON, DAVID MOWRY, PHIL
ORTIZ, MIKE ROTE, ERICK TRAN, CHRIS UNGAR, CINDY VANCE, STEVE VANCE

Contributing Writers:
IAN BOOTHBY, SCOTT M. GIMPLE, ROB HAMMERSLEY, JIM LINCOLN, BILL
MORRISON, JEFF ROSENTHAL, BILLY RUBENSTEIN, DAN STUDNEY

CONTENTS

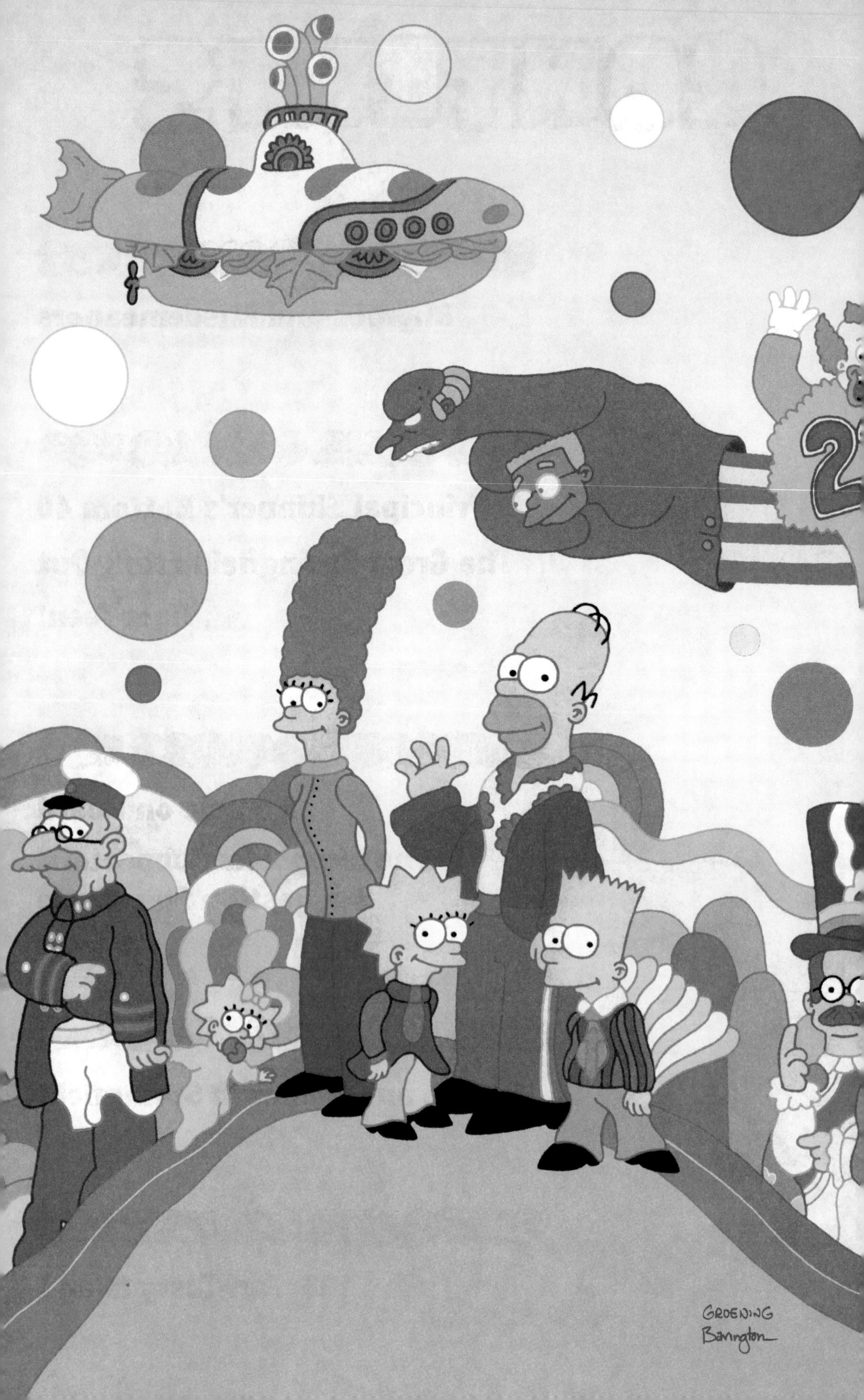
GROENING
Barrington

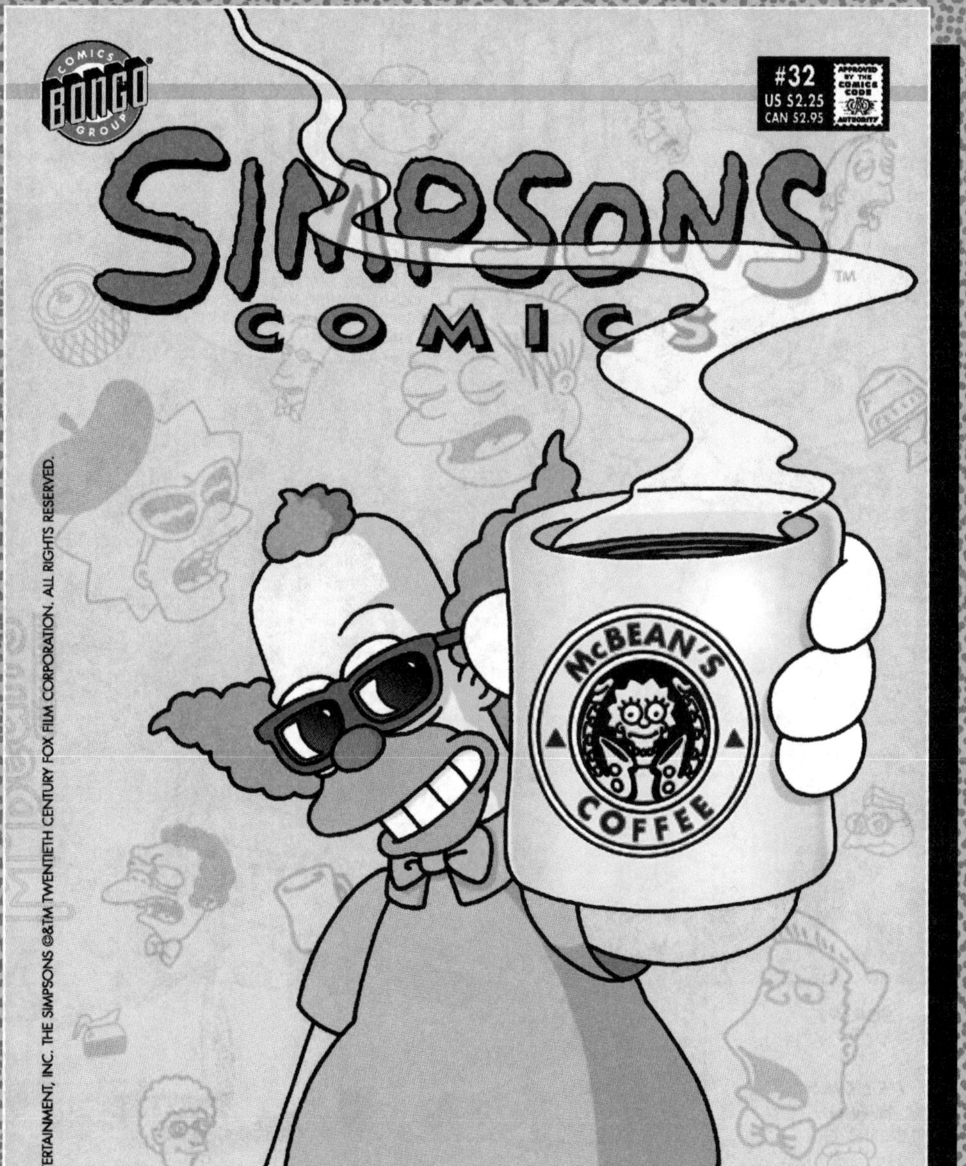

BONGO COMICS GROUP
#32
US $2.25
CAN $2.95
APPROVED BY THE COMICS CODE AUTHORITY
SIMPSONS COMICS
McBEAN'S COFFEE
©1997 BONGO ENTERTAINMENT, INC. THE SIMPSONS ©&TM TWENTIETH CENTURY FOX FILM CORPORATION. ALL RIGHTS RESERVED.
GROENING

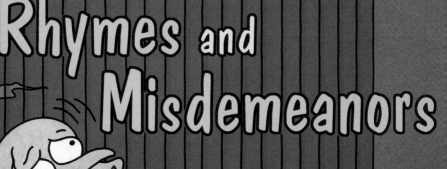

Rhymes and Misdemeanors

¡GASP¡ SMITHERS, COME QUICKLY! SOME BUMPTIOUS INSURRECTIONIST HAS *POISONED* ME!

SCRIPT
JEFF ROSENTHAL

PENCILS
TIM BAVINGTON
STEPHANIE GLADDEN
PHIL ORTIZ

INKS
TIM BAVINGTON
BILL MORRISON

LETTERS
JEANNINE BLACK

COLORS
NATHAN KANE

LIGHT, NO SUGAR
MATT GROENING

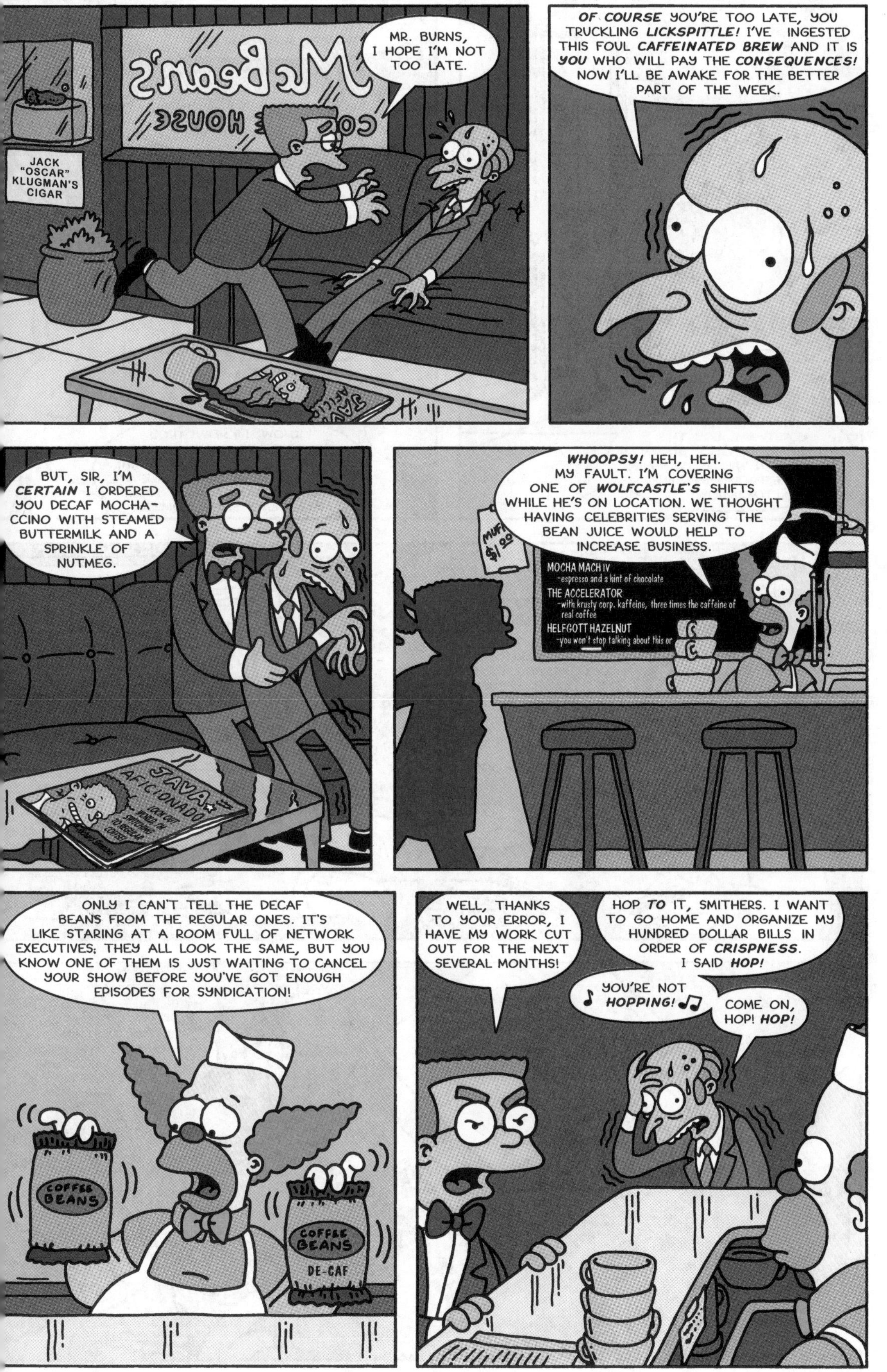

JACK "OSCAR" KLUGMAN'S CIGAR
MR. BURNS, I HOPE I'M NOT TOO LATE.
OF COURSE YOU'RE TOO LATE, YOU TRUCKLING ***LICKSPITTLE!*** I'VE INGESTED THIS FOUL ***CAFFEINATED BREW*** AND IT IS ***YOU*** WHO WILL PAY THE ***CONSEQUENCES!*** NOW I'LL BE AWAKE FOR THE BETTER PART OF THE WEEK.
BUT, SIR, I'M ***CERTAIN*** I ORDERED YOU DECAF MOCHA-CCINO WITH STEAMED BUTTERMILK AND A SPRINKLE OF NUTMEG.
JAVA AFICIONADO
LOOK OUT WORLD, I'M SWITCHING TO REGULAR COFFEE!
WHOOPSY! HEH, HEH. MY FAULT. I'M COVERING ONE OF ***WOLFCASTLE'S*** SHIFTS WHILE HE'S ON LOCATION. WE THOUGHT HAVING CELEBRITIES SERVING THE BEAN JUICE WOULD HELP TO INCREASE BUSINESS.
MOCHA MACH IV
-espresso and a hint of chocolate
THE ACCELERATOR
-with krusty corp. kaffeine, three times the caffeine of real coffee
HELFGOTT HAZELNUT
-you won't stop talking about this or
ONLY I CAN'T TELL THE DECAF BEANS FROM THE REGULAR ONES. IT'S LIKE STARING AT A ROOM FULL OF NETWORK EXECUTIVES; THEY ALL LOOK THE SAME, BUT YOU KNOW ONE OF THEM IS JUST WAITING TO CANCEL YOUR SHOW BEFORE YOU'VE GOT ENOUGH EPISODES FOR SYNDICATION!
COFFEE BEANS
COFFEE BEANS
DE-CAF
WELL, THANKS TO YOUR ERROR, I HAVE MY WORK CUT OUT FOR THE NEXT SEVERAL MONTHS!
HOP ***TO*** IT, SMITHERS. I WANT TO GO HOME AND ORGANIZE MY HUNDRED DOLLAR BILLS IN ORDER OF ***CRISPNESS***. I SAID ***HOP!***
♪ YOU'RE NOT ***HOPPING!*** ♫
COME ON, HOP! ***HOP!***

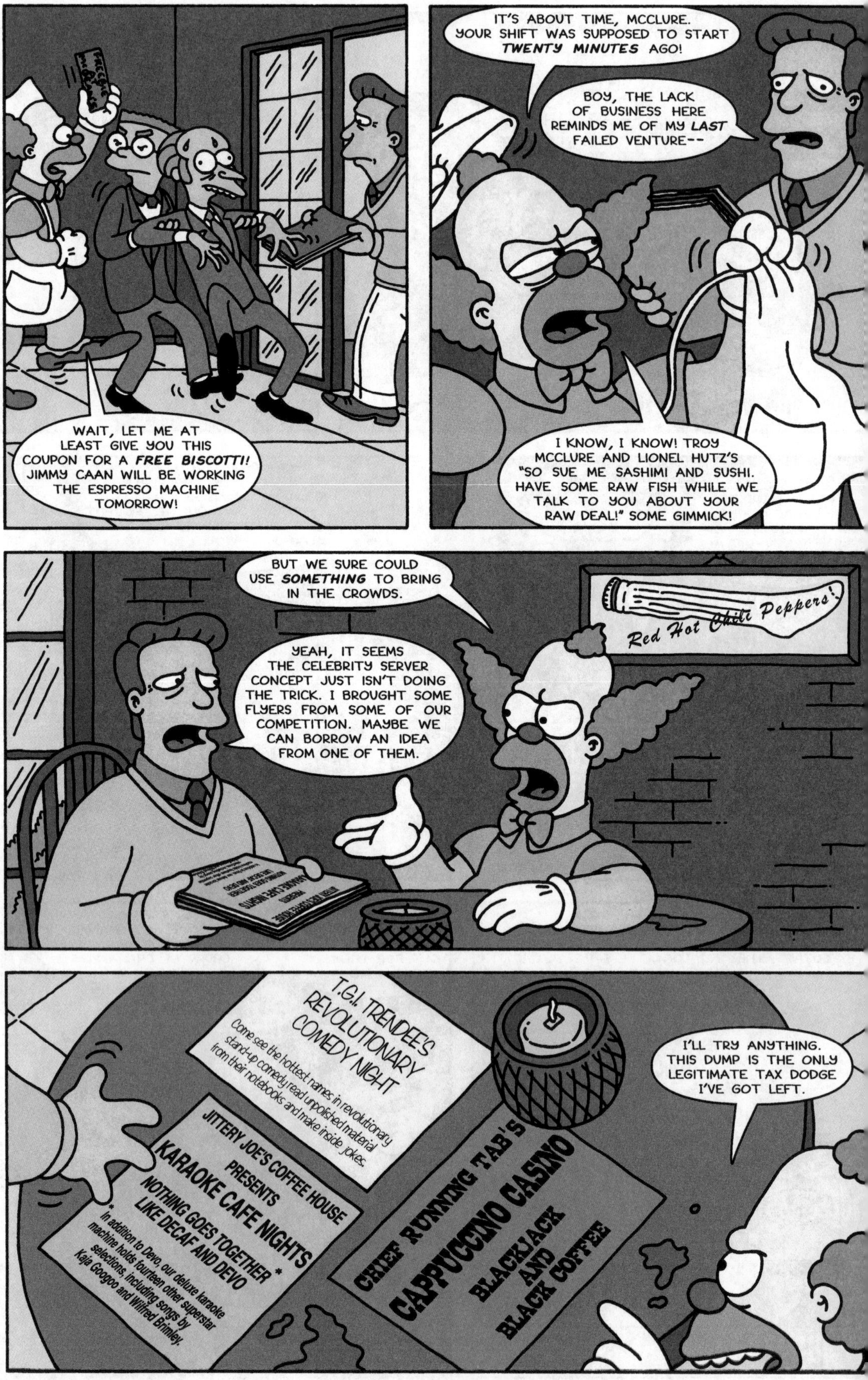
WAIT, LET ME AT LEAST GIVE YOU THIS COUPON FOR A ***FREE BISCOTTI***! JIMMY CAAN WILL BE WORKING THE ESPRESSO MACHINE TOMORROW!
IT'S ABOUT TIME, MCCLURE. YOUR SHIFT WAS SUPPOSED TO START ***TWENTY MINUTES*** AGO!
BOY, THE LACK OF BUSINESS HERE REMINDS ME OF MY ***LAST*** FAILED VENTURE--
I KNOW, I KNOW! TROY MCCLURE AND LIONEL HUTZ'S "SO SUE ME SASHIMI AND SUSHI. HAVE SOME RAW FISH WHILE WE TALK TO YOU ABOUT YOUR RAW DEAL!" SOME GIMMICK!
BUT WE SURE COULD USE ***SOMETHING*** TO BRING IN THE CROWDS.
YEAH, IT SEEMS THE CELEBRITY SERVER CONCEPT JUST ISN'T DOING THE TRICK. I BROUGHT SOME FLYERS FROM SOME OF OUR COMPETITION. MAYBE WE CAN BORROW AN IDEA FROM ONE OF THEM.
Red Hot Chili Peppers
T.G.I. TRENDEE'S REVOLUTIONARY COMEDY NIGHT
Come see the hottest names in revolutionary stand-up comedy read unpolished material from their notebooks and make inside jokes.
JITTERY JOE'S COFFEE HOUSE PRESENTS
KARAOKE CAFE NIGHTS
NOTHING GOES TOGETHER LIKE DECAF AND DEVO *
* In addition to Devo, our deluxe karaoke machine holds fourteen other superstar selections, including songs by Kaja Googoo and Wilfred Brimley.
CHIEF RUNNING TAB'S
CAPPUCCINO CASINO
BLACKJACK AND BLACK COFFEE
I'LL TRY ANYTHING. THIS DUMP IS THE ONLY LEGITIMATE TAX DODGE I'VE GOT LEFT.

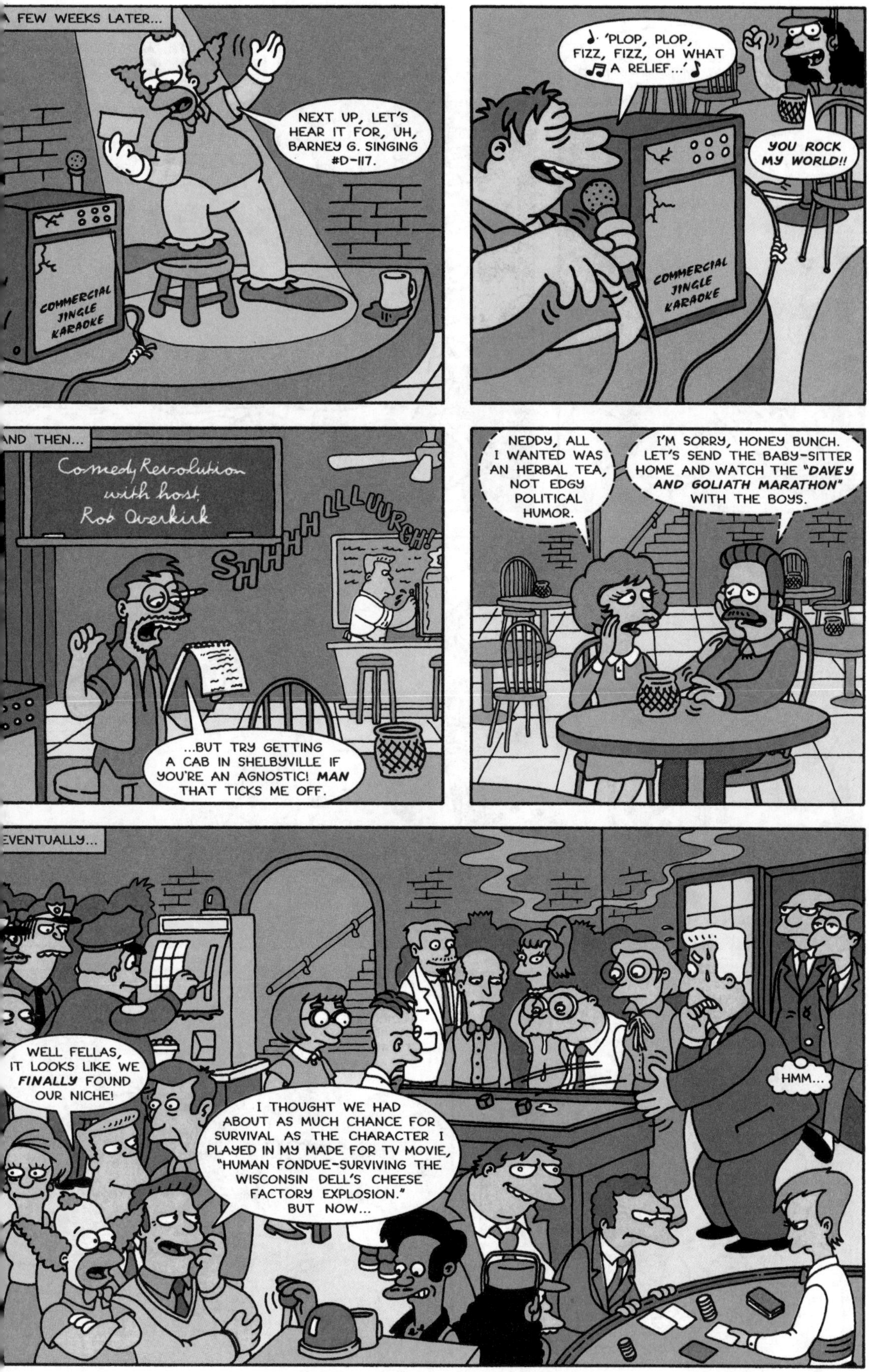
A FEW WEEKS LATER...
NEXT UP, LET'S HEAR IT FOR, UH, BARNEY G. SINGING #D-117.
COMMERCIAL JINGLE KARAOKE
'PLOP, PLOP, FIZZ, FIZZ, OH WHAT A RELIEF...'
YOU ROCK MY WORLD!!
COMMERCIAL JINGLE KARAOKE
AND THEN...
Comedy Revolution with host Rob Overkirk
SHHHHH
LLLUURGH!
...BUT TRY GETTING A CAB IN SHELBYVILLE IF YOU'RE AN AGNOSTIC! MAN THAT TICKS ME OFF.
NEDDY, ALL I WANTED WAS AN HERBAL TEA, NOT EDGY POLITICAL HUMOR.
I'M SORRY, HONEY BUNCH. LET'S SEND THE BABY-SITTER HOME AND WATCH THE "DAVEY AND GOLIATH MARATHON" WITH THE BOYS.
EVENTUALLY...
WELL FELLAS, IT LOOKS LIKE WE FINALLY FOUND OUR NICHE!
I THOUGHT WE HAD ABOUT AS MUCH CHANCE FOR SURVIVAL AS THE CHARACTER I PLAYED IN MY MADE FOR TV MOVIE, "HUMAN FONDUE-SURVIVING THE WISCONSIN DELL'S CHEESE FACTORY EXPLOSION." BUT NOW...
HMM...

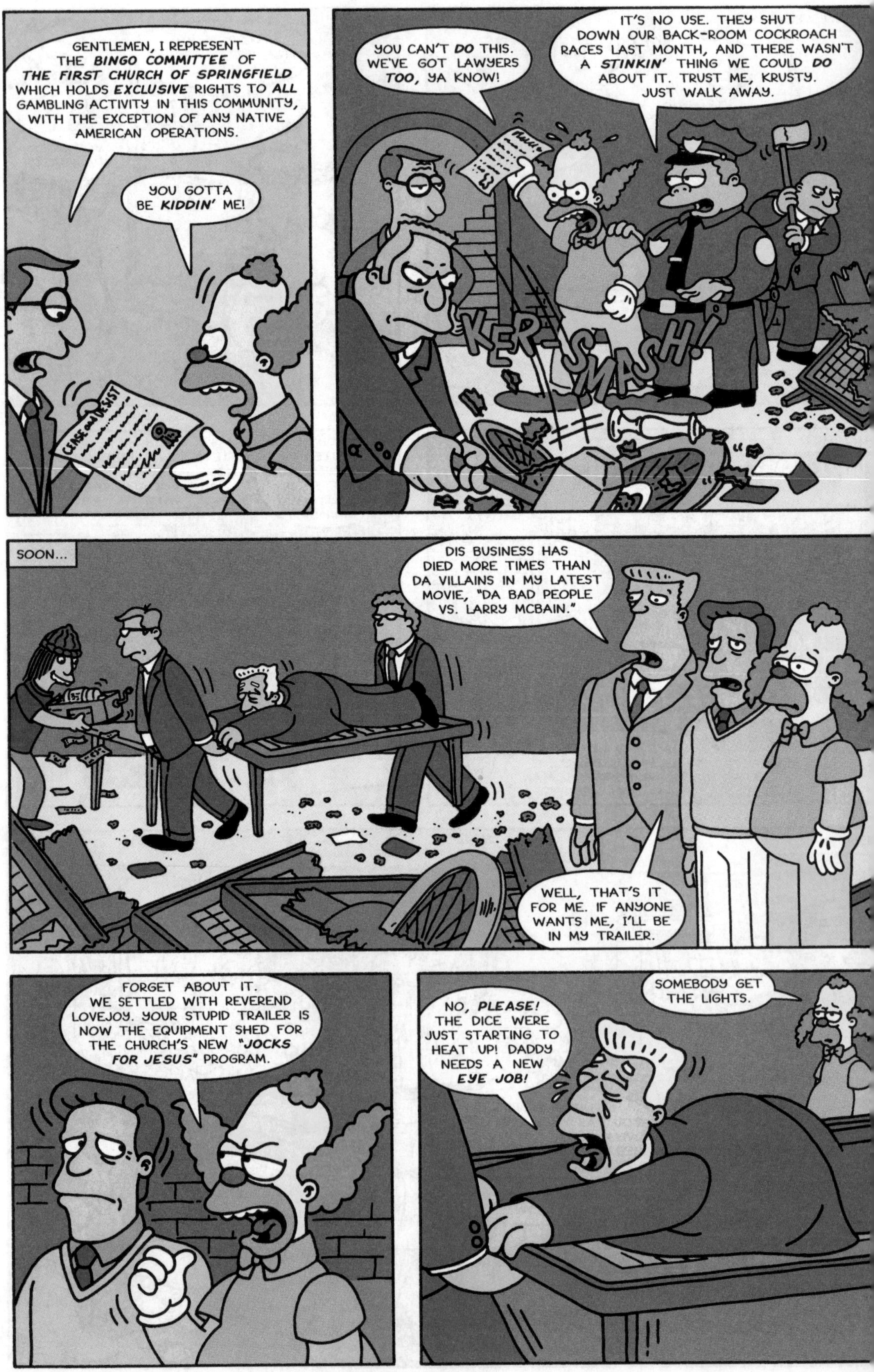
GENTLEMEN, I REPRESENT THE BINGO COMMITTEE OF THE FIRST CHURCH OF SPRINGFIELD WHICH HOLDS EXCLUSIVE RIGHTS TO ALL GAMBLING ACTIVITY IN THIS COMMUNITY, WITH THE EXCEPTION OF ANY NATIVE AMERICAN OPERATIONS.
CEASE and DESIST
YOU GOTTA BE KIDDIN' ME!
YOU CAN'T DO THIS. WE'VE GOT LAWYERS TOO, YA KNOW!
IT'S NO USE. THEY SHUT DOWN OUR BACK-ROOM COCKROACH RACES LAST MONTH, AND THERE WASN'T A STINKIN' THING WE COULD DO ABOUT IT. TRUST ME, KRUSTY. JUST WALK AWAY.
KER-SMASH!
SOON...
DIS BUSINESS HAS DIED MORE TIMES THAN DA VILLAINS IN MY LATEST MOVIE, "DA BAD PEOPLE VS. LARRY MCBAIN."
WELL, THAT'S IT FOR ME. IF ANYONE WANTS ME, I'LL BE IN MY TRAILER.
FORGET ABOUT IT. WE SETTLED WITH REVEREND LOVEJOY. YOUR STUPID TRAILER IS NOW THE EQUIPMENT SHED FOR THE CHURCH'S NEW "JOCKS FOR JESUS" PROGRAM.
NO, PLEASE! THE DICE WERE JUST STARTING TO HEAT UP! DADDY NEEDS A NEW EYE JOB!
SOMEBODY GET THE LIGHTS.

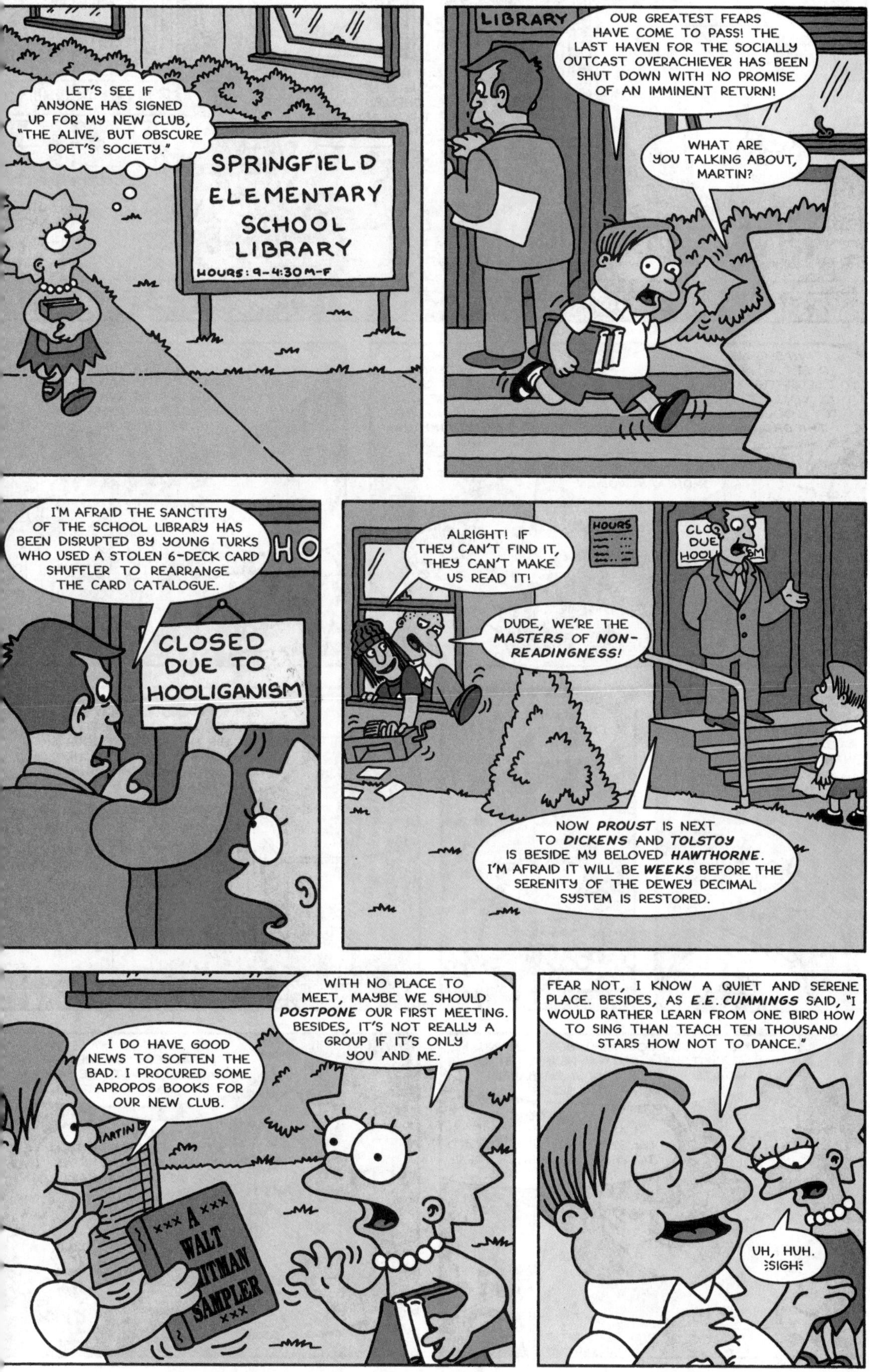

LET'S SEE IF ANYONE HAS SIGNED UP FOR MY NEW CLUB, "THE ALIVE, BUT OBSCURE POET'S SOCIETY."
SPRINGFIELD ELEMENTARY SCHOOL LIBRARY
HOURS: 9–4:30 M–F
LIBRARY
OUR GREATEST FEARS HAVE COME TO PASS! THE LAST HAVEN FOR THE SOCIALLY OUTCAST OVERACHIEVER HAS BEEN SHUT DOWN WITH NO PROMISE OF AN IMMINENT RETURN!
WHAT ARE YOU TALKING ABOUT, MARTIN?
I'M AFRAID THE SANCTITY OF THE SCHOOL LIBRARY HAS BEEN DISRUPTED BY YOUNG TURKS WHO USED A STOLEN 6-DECK CARD SHUFFLER TO REARRANGE THE CARD CATALOGUE.
CLOSED DUE TO HOOLIGANISM
ALRIGHT! IF THEY CAN'T FIND IT, THEY CAN'T MAKE US READ IT!
DUDE, WE'RE THE MASTERS OF NON-READINGNESS!
HOURS
NOW PROUST IS NEXT TO DICKENS AND TOLSTOY IS BESIDE MY BELOVED HAWTHORNE. I'M AFRAID IT WILL BE WEEKS BEFORE THE SERENITY OF THE DEWEY DECIMAL SYSTEM IS RESTORED.
I DO HAVE GOOD NEWS TO SOFTEN THE BAD. I PROCURED SOME APROPOS BOOKS FOR OUR NEW CLUB.
A WALT WHITMAN SAMPLER
WITH NO PLACE TO MEET, MAYBE WE SHOULD POSTPONE OUR FIRST MEETING. BESIDES, IT'S NOT REALLY A GROUP IF IT'S ONLY YOU AND ME.
FEAR NOT, I KNOW A QUIET AND SERENE PLACE. BESIDES, AS E.E. CUMMINGS SAID, "I WOULD RATHER LEARN FROM ONE BIRD HOW TO SING THAN TEACH TEN THOUSAND STARS HOW NOT TO DANCE."
UH, HUH. SIGH

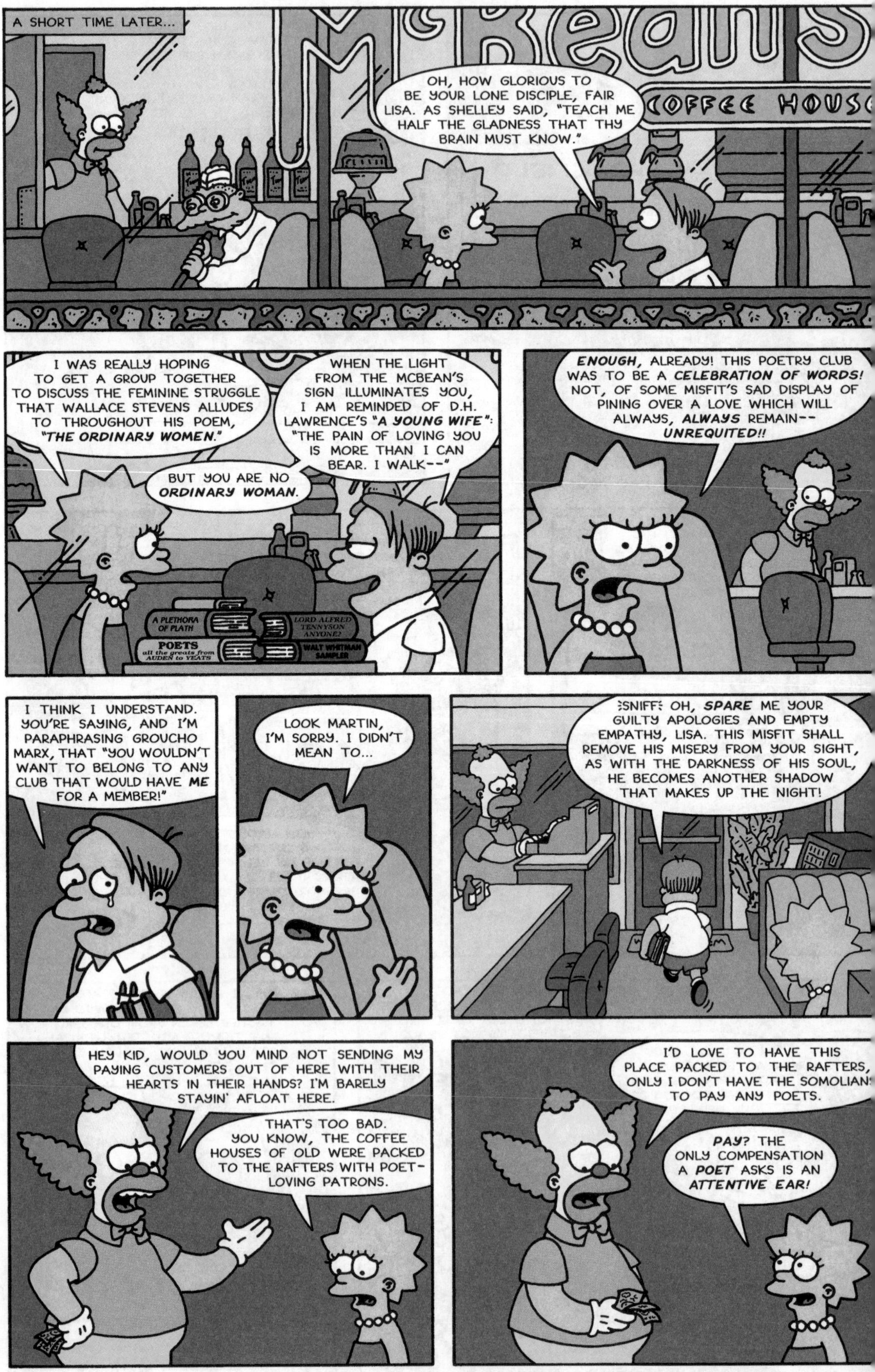
A SHORT TIME LATER...
McBean's
COFFEE HOUS
OH, HOW GLORIOUS TO BE YOUR LONE DISCIPLE, FAIR LISA. AS SHELLEY SAID, "TEACH ME HALF THE GLADNESS THAT THY BRAIN MUST KNOW."
I WAS REALLY HOPING TO GET A GROUP TOGETHER TO DISCUSS THE FEMININE STRUGGLE THAT WALLACE STEVENS ALLUDES TO THROUGHOUT HIS POEM, "THE ORDINARY WOMEN."
BUT YOU ARE NO ORDINARY WOMAN.
WHEN THE LIGHT FROM THE MCBEAN'S SIGN ILLUMINATES YOU, I AM REMINDED OF D.H. LAWRENCE'S "A YOUNG WIFE": "THE PAIN OF LOVING YOU IS MORE THAN I CAN BEAR. I WALK--"
A PLETHORA OF PLATH
POETS all the greats from AUDEN to YEATS
LORD ALFRED TENNYSON ANYONE?
WALT WHITMAN SAMPLER
ENOUGH, ALREADY! THIS POETRY CLUB WAS TO BE A CELEBRATION OF WORDS! NOT, OF SOME MISFIT'S SAD DISPLAY OF PINING OVER A LOVE WHICH WILL ALWAYS, ALWAYS REMAIN-- UNREQUITED!!
I THINK I UNDERSTAND. YOU'RE SAYING, AND I'M PARAPHRASING GROUCHO MARX, THAT "YOU WOULDN'T WANT TO BELONG TO ANY CLUB THAT WOULD HAVE ME FOR A MEMBER!"
LOOK MARTIN, I'M SORRY. I DIDN'T MEAN TO...
SNIFF OH, SPARE ME YOUR GUILTY APOLOGIES AND EMPTY EMPATHY, LISA. THIS MISFIT SHALL REMOVE HIS MISERY FROM YOUR SIGHT, AS WITH THE DARKNESS OF HIS SOUL, HE BECOMES ANOTHER SHADOW THAT MAKES UP THE NIGHT!
HEY KID, WOULD YOU MIND NOT SENDING MY PAYING CUSTOMERS OUT OF HERE WITH THEIR HEARTS IN THEIR HANDS? I'M BARELY STAYIN' AFLOAT HERE.
THAT'S TOO BAD. YOU KNOW, THE COFFEE HOUSES OF OLD WERE PACKED TO THE RAFTERS WITH POET-LOVING PATRONS.
I'D LOVE TO HAVE THIS PLACE PACKED TO THE RAFTERS, ONLY I DON'T HAVE THE SOMOLIANS TO PAY ANY POETS.
PAY? THE ONLY COMPENSATION A POET ASKS IS AN ATTENTIVE EAR!

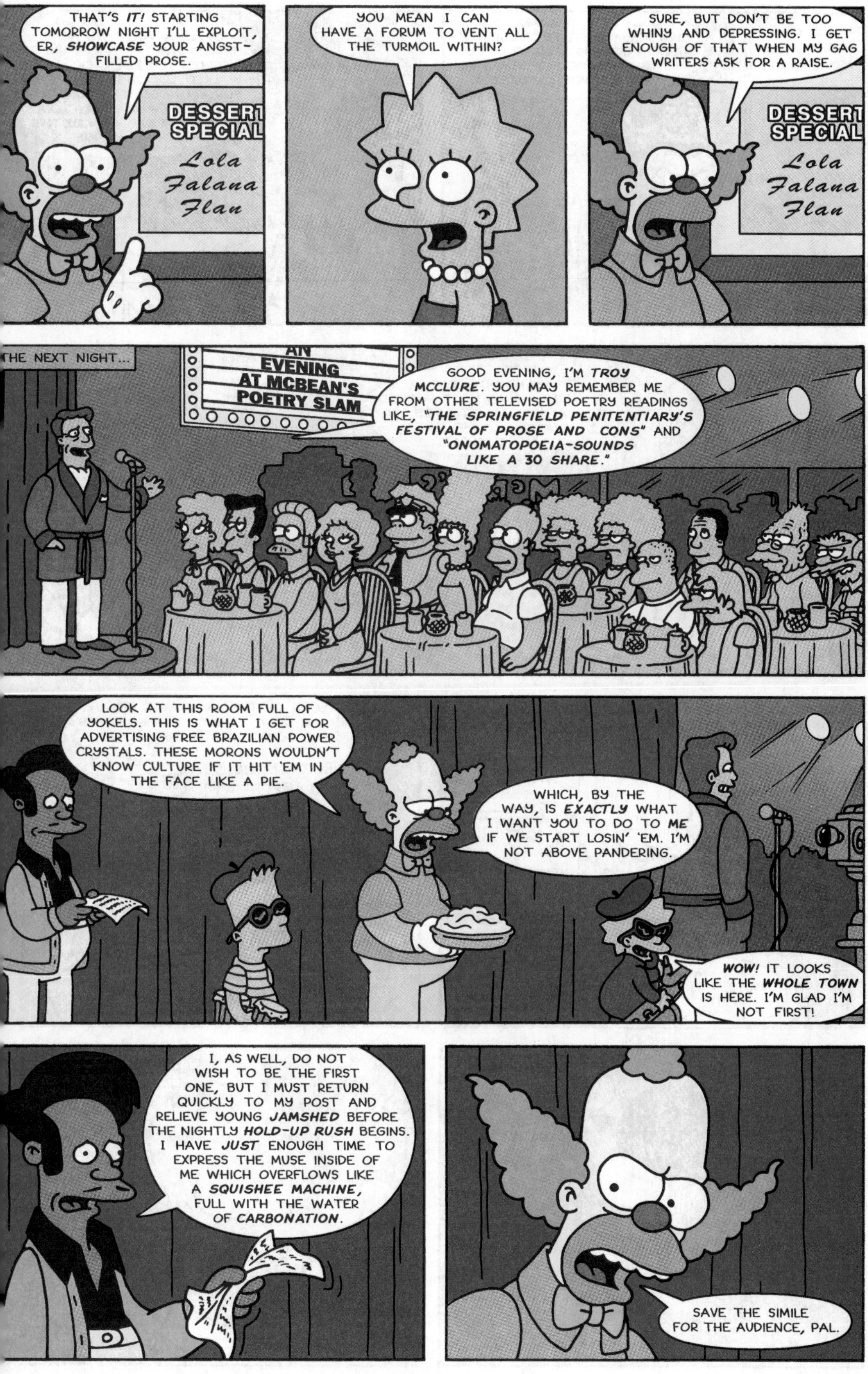
THAT'S IT! STARTING TOMORROW NIGHT I'LL EXPLOIT, ER, SHOWCASE YOUR ANGST-FILLED PROSE.
DESSERT SPECIAL Lola Falana Flan
YOU MEAN I CAN HAVE A FORUM TO VENT ALL THE TURMOIL WITHIN?
SURE, BUT DON'T BE TOO WHINY AND DEPRESSING. I GET ENOUGH OF THAT WHEN MY GAG WRITERS ASK FOR A RAISE.
DESSERT SPECIAL Lola Falana Flan
THE NEXT NIGHT...
AN EVENING AT MCBEAN'S POETRY SLAM
GOOD EVENING, I'M TROY MCCLURE. YOU MAY REMEMBER ME FROM OTHER TELEVISED POETRY READINGS LIKE, "THE SPRINGFIELD PENITENTIARY'S FESTIVAL OF PROSE AND CONS" AND "ONOMATOPOEIA-SOUNDS LIKE A 30 SHARE."
LOOK AT THIS ROOM FULL OF YOKELS. THIS IS WHAT I GET FOR ADVERTISING FREE BRAZILIAN POWER CRYSTALS. THESE MORONS WOULDN'T KNOW CULTURE IF IT HIT 'EM IN THE FACE LIKE A PIE.
WHICH, BY THE WAY, IS EXACTLY WHAT I WANT YOU TO DO TO ME IF WE START LOSIN' 'EM. I'M NOT ABOVE PANDERING.
WOW! IT LOOKS LIKE THE WHOLE TOWN IS HERE. I'M GLAD I'M NOT FIRST!
I, AS WELL, DO NOT WISH TO BE THE FIRST ONE, BUT I MUST RETURN QUICKLY TO MY POST AND RELIEVE YOUNG JAMSHED BEFORE THE NIGHTLY HOLD-UP RUSH BEGINS. I HAVE JUST ENOUGH TIME TO EXPRESS THE MUSE INSIDE OF ME WHICH OVERFLOWS LIKE A SQUISHEE MACHINE, FULL WITH THE WATER OF CARBONATION.
SAVE THE SIMILE FOR THE AUDIENCE, PAL.

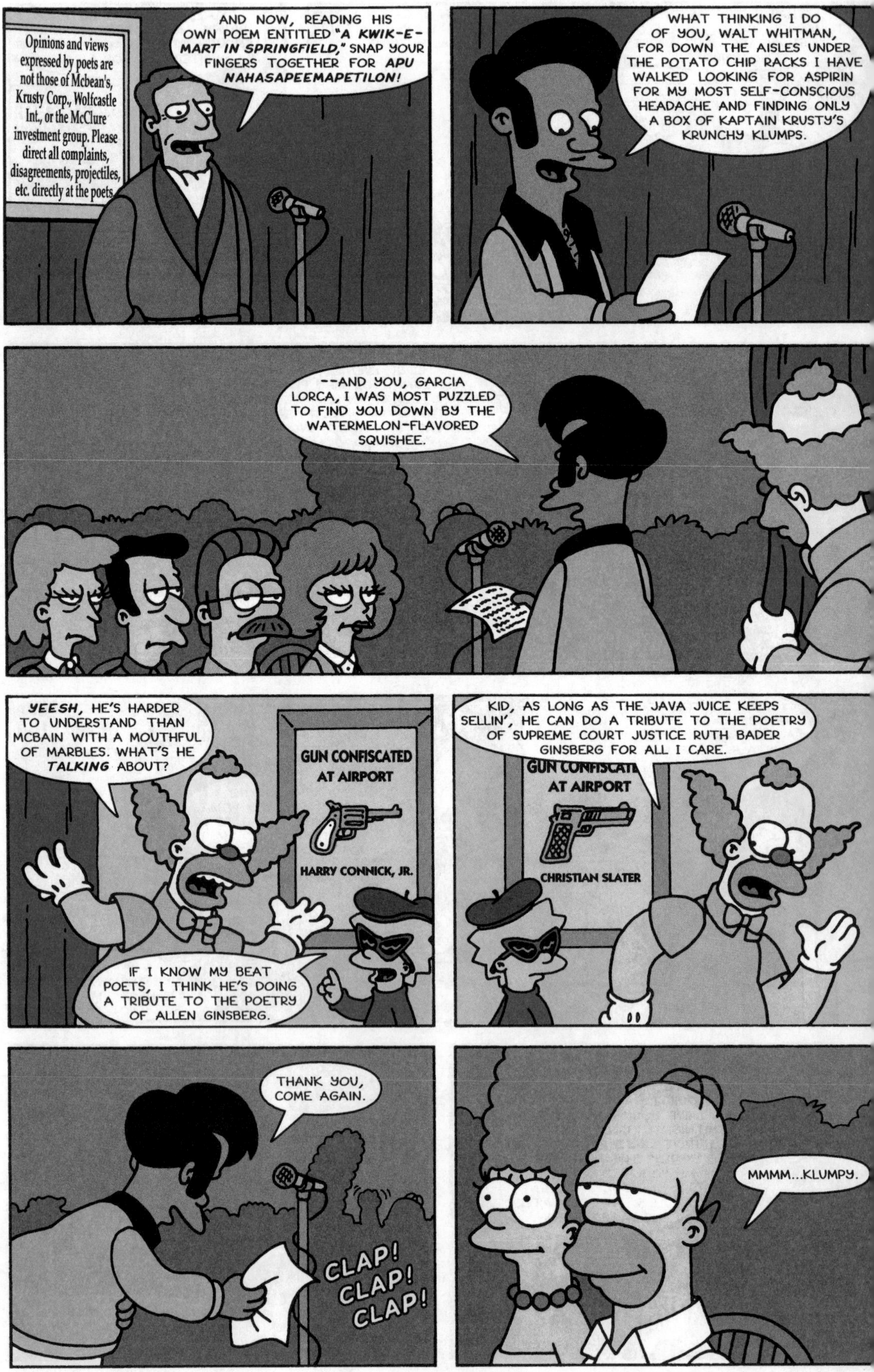
Opinions and views expressed by poets are not those of Mcbean's, Krusty Corp., Wolfcastle Int., or the McClure investment group. Please direct all complaints, disagreements, projectiles, etc. directly at the poets.
AND NOW, READING HIS OWN POEM ENTITLED "A KWIK-E-MART IN SPRINGFIELD," SNAP YOUR FINGERS TOGETHER FOR APU NAHASAPEEMAPETILON!
WHAT THINKING I DO OF YOU, WALT WHITMAN, FOR DOWN THE AISLES UNDER THE POTATO CHIP RACKS I HAVE WALKED LOOKING FOR ASPIRIN FOR MY MOST SELF-CONSCIOUS HEADACHE AND FINDING ONLY A BOX OF KAPTAIN KRUSTY'S KRUNCHY KLUMPS.
--AND YOU, GARCIA LORCA, I WAS MOST PUZZLED TO FIND YOU DOWN BY THE WATERMELON-FLAVORED SQUISHEE.
YEESH, HE'S HARDER TO UNDERSTAND THAN MCBAIN WITH A MOUTHFUL OF MARBLES. WHAT'S HE TALKING ABOUT?
GUN CONFISCATED AT AIRPORT
HARRY CONNICK, JR.
IF I KNOW MY BEAT POETS, I THINK HE'S DOING A TRIBUTE TO THE POETRY OF ALLEN GINSBERG.
KID, AS LONG AS THE JAVA JUICE KEEPS SELLIN', HE CAN DO A TRIBUTE TO THE POETRY OF SUPREME COURT JUSTICE RUTH BADER GINSBERG FOR ALL I CARE.
GUN CONFISCATE AT AIRPORT
CHRISTIAN SLATER
THANK YOU, COME AGAIN.
CLAP! CLAP! CLAP!
MMMM...KLUMPY.

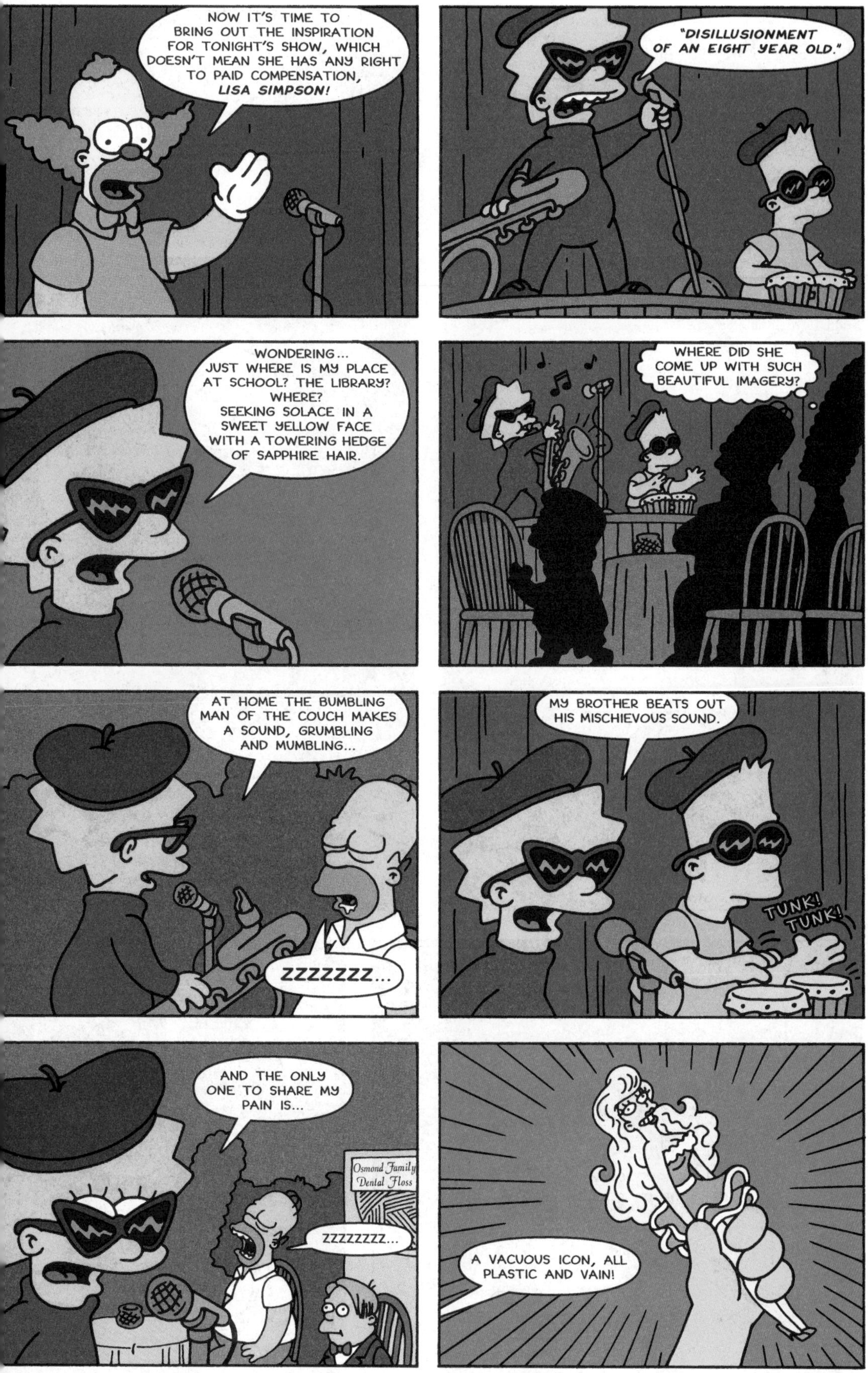
NOW IT'S TIME TO BRING OUT THE INSPIRATION FOR TONIGHT'S SHOW, WHICH DOESN'T MEAN SHE HAS ANY RIGHT TO PAID COMPENSATION, LISA SIMPSON!
"DISILLUSIONMENT OF AN EIGHT YEAR OLD."
WONDERING... JUST WHERE IS MY PLACE AT SCHOOL? THE LIBRARY? WHERE? SEEKING SOLACE IN A SWEET YELLOW FACE WITH A TOWERING HEDGE OF SAPPHIRE HAIR.
WHERE DID SHE COME UP WITH SUCH BEAUTIFUL IMAGERY?
AT HOME THE BUMBLING MAN OF THE COUCH MAKES A SOUND, GRUMBLING AND MUMBLING...
ZZZZZZZ...
MY BROTHER BEATS OUT HIS MISCHIEVOUS SOUND.
TUNK! TUNK!
AND THE ONLY ONE TO SHARE MY PAIN IS...
Osmond Family Dental Floss
ZZZZZZZZ...
A VACUOUS ICON, ALL PLASTIC AND VAIN!

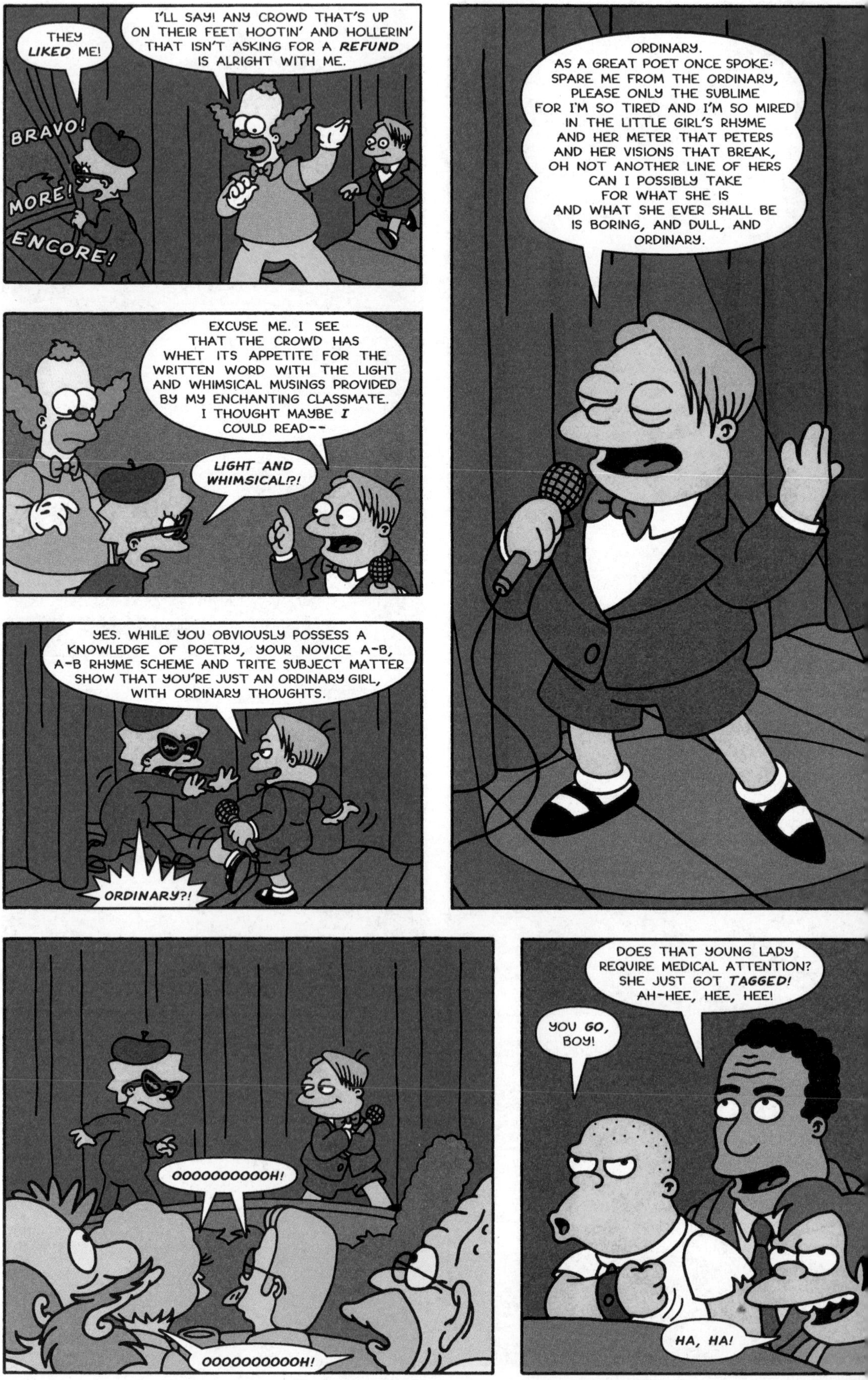
THEY LIKED ME!
I'LL SAY! ANY CROWD THAT'S UP ON THEIR FEET HOOTIN' AND HOLLERIN' THAT ISN'T ASKING FOR A REFUND IS ALRIGHT WITH ME.
BRAVO!
MORE!
ENCORE!
EXCUSE ME. I SEE THAT THE CROWD HAS WHET ITS APPETITE FOR THE WRITTEN WORD WITH THE LIGHT AND WHIMSICAL MUSINGS PROVIDED BY MY ENCHANTING CLASSMATE. I THOUGHT MAYBE I COULD READ--
LIGHT AND WHIMSICAL!?!
YES. WHILE YOU OBVIOUSLY POSSESS A KNOWLEDGE OF POETRY, YOUR NOVICE A-B, A-B RHYME SCHEME AND TRITE SUBJECT MATTER SHOW THAT YOU'RE JUST AN ORDINARY GIRL, WITH ORDINARY THOUGHTS.
ORDINARY?!
ORDINARY. AS A GREAT POET ONCE SPOKE: SPARE ME FROM THE ORDINARY, PLEASE ONLY THE SUBLIME FOR I'M SO TIRED AND I'M SO MIRED IN THE LITTLE GIRL'S RHYME AND HER METER THAT PETERS AND HER VISIONS THAT BREAK, OH NOT ANOTHER LINE OF HERS CAN I POSSIBLY TAKE FOR WHAT SHE IS AND WHAT SHE EVER SHALL BE IS BORING, AND DULL, AND ORDINARY.
OOOOOOOOOOH!
OOOOOOOOOOH!
DOES THAT YOUNG LADY REQUIRE MEDICAL ATTENTION? SHE JUST GOT TAGGED! AH-HEE, HEE, HEE!
YOU GO, BOY!
HA, HA!

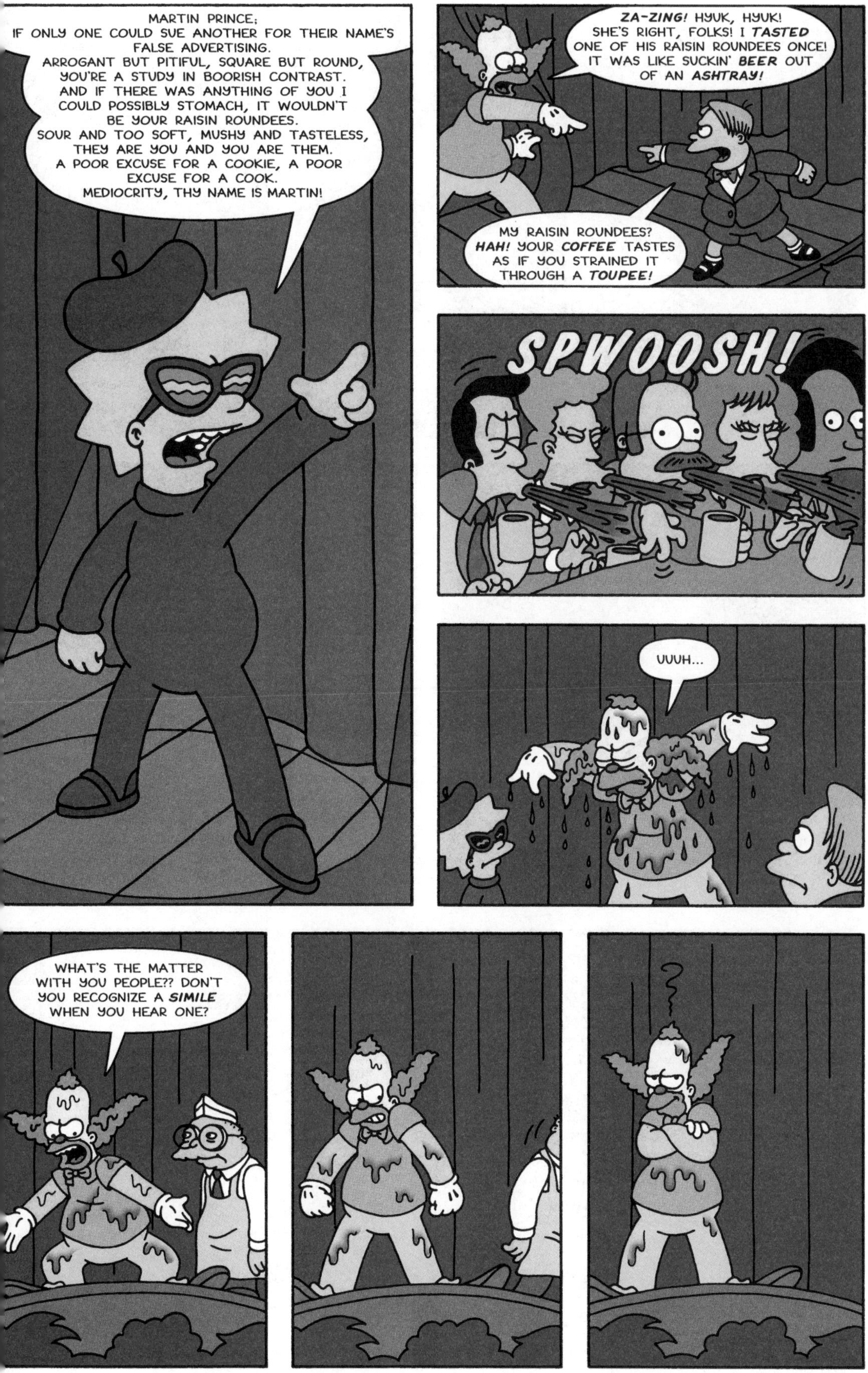

MARTIN PRINCE; IF ONLY ONE COULD SUE ANOTHER FOR THEIR NAME'S FALSE ADVERTISING. ARROGANT BUT PITIFUL, SQUARE BUT ROUND, YOU'RE A STUDY IN BOORISH CONTRAST. AND IF THERE WAS ANYTHING OF YOU I COULD POSSIBLY STOMACH, IT WOULDN'T BE YOUR RAISIN ROUNDEES. SOUR AND TOO SOFT, MUSHY AND TASTELESS, THEY ARE YOU AND YOU ARE THEM. A POOR EXCUSE FOR A COOKIE, A POOR EXCUSE FOR A COOK. MEDIOCRITY, THY NAME IS MARTIN!
ZA-ZING! HYUK, HYUK! SHE'S RIGHT, FOLKS! I TASTED ONE OF HIS RAISIN ROUNDEES ONCE! IT WAS LIKE SUCKIN' BEER OUT OF AN ASHTRAY!
MY RAISIN ROUNDEES? HAH! YOUR COFFEE TASTES AS IF YOU STRAINED IT THROUGH A TOUPEE!
SPWOOSH!
UUUH...
WHAT'S THE MATTER WITH YOU PEOPLE?? DON'T YOU RECOGNIZE A SIMILE WHEN YOU HEAR ONE?
?

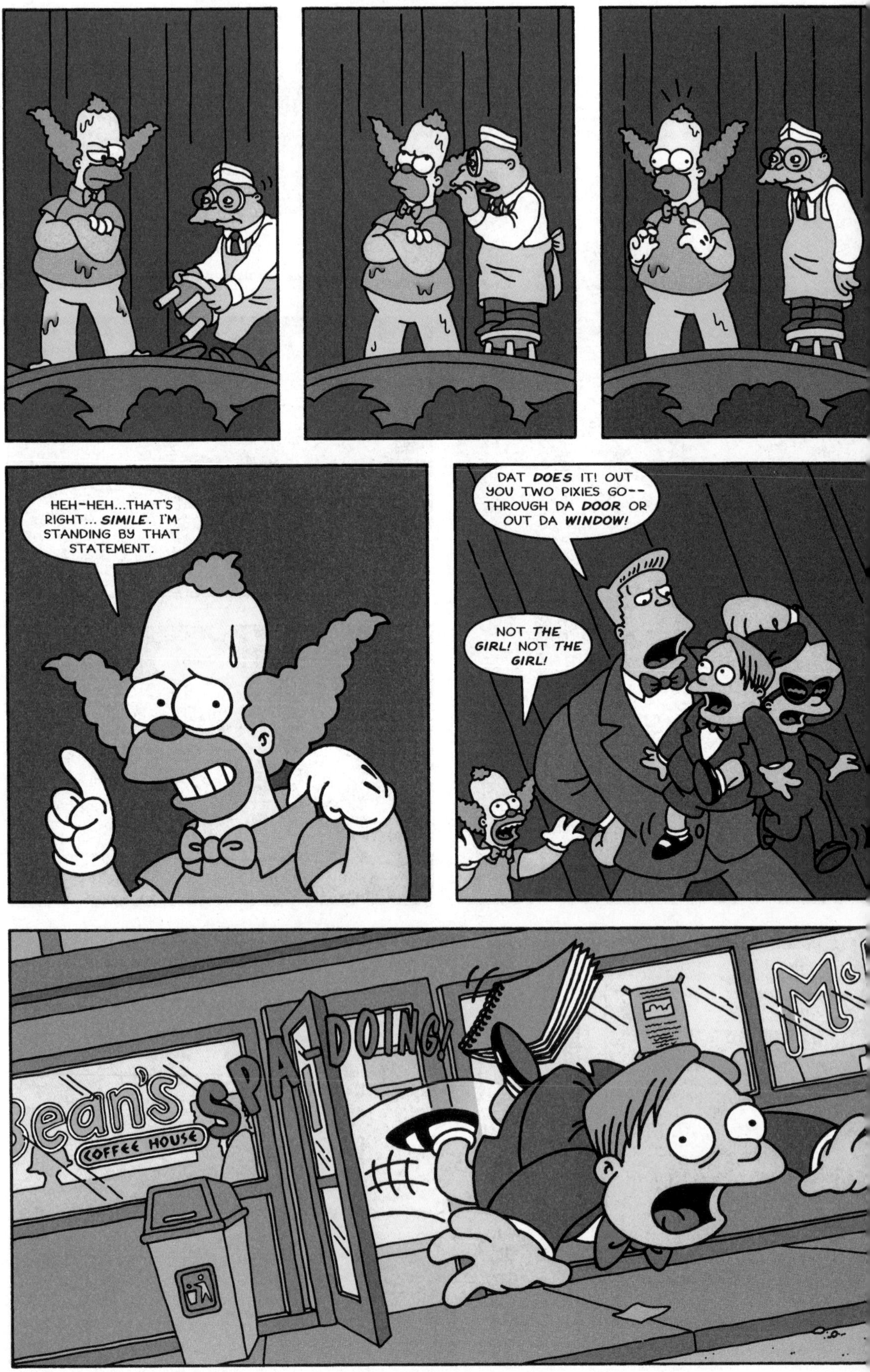
HEH-HEH...THAT'S RIGHT... SIMILE. I'M STANDING BY THAT STATEMENT.
DAT DOES IT! OUT YOU TWO PIXIES GO-- THROUGH DA DOOR OR OUT DA WINDOW!
NOT THE GIRL! NOT THE GIRL!
SPA-DOING!
Bean's
COFFEE HOUSE

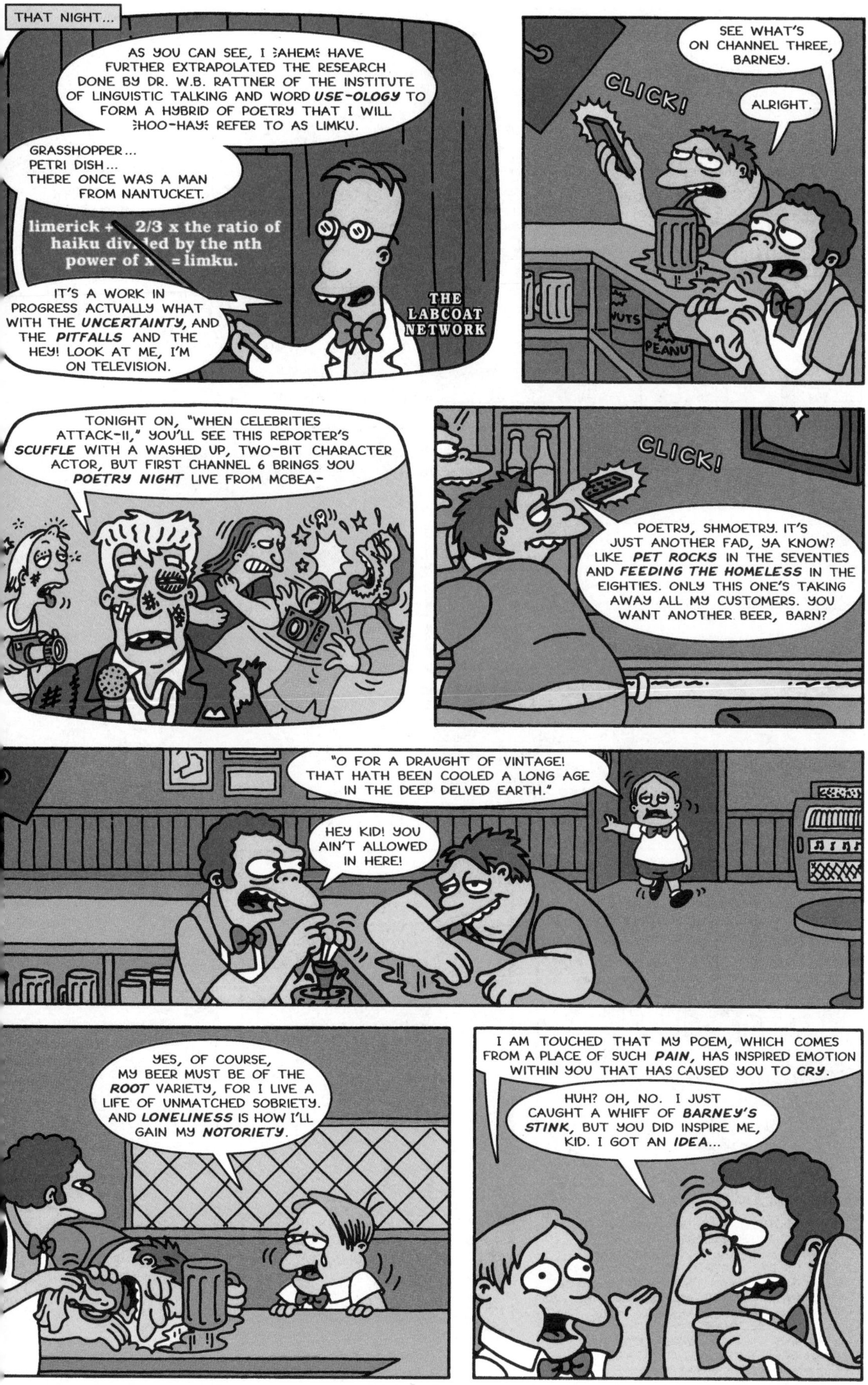
THAT NIGHT...
AS YOU CAN SEE, I :AHEM: HAVE FURTHER EXTRAPOLATED THE RESEARCH DONE BY DR. W.B. RATTNER OF THE INSTITUTE OF LINGUISTIC TALKING AND WORD USE-OLOGY TO FORM A HYBRID OF POETRY THAT I WILL :HOO-HAY: REFER TO AS LIMKU.
GRASSHOPPER... PETRI DISH... THERE ONCE WAS A MAN FROM NANTUCKET.
limerick + 2/3 x the ratio of haiku divided by the nth power of x = limku.
IT'S A WORK IN PROGRESS ACTUALLY WHAT WITH THE UNCERTAINTY, AND THE PITFALLS AND THE HEY! LOOK AT ME, I'M ON TELEVISION.
THE LABCOAT NETWORK
SEE WHAT'S ON CHANNEL THREE, BARNEY.
CLICK!
ALRIGHT.
TONIGHT ON, "WHEN CELEBRITIES ATTACK-II," YOU'LL SEE THIS REPORTER'S SCUFFLE WITH A WASHED UP, TWO-BIT CHARACTER ACTOR, BUT FIRST CHANNEL 6 BRINGS YOU POETRY NIGHT LIVE FROM MCBEA-
CLICK!
POETRY, SHMOETRY. IT'S JUST ANOTHER FAD, YA KNOW? LIKE PET ROCKS IN THE SEVENTIES AND FEEDING THE HOMELESS IN THE EIGHTIES. ONLY THIS ONE'S TAKING AWAY ALL MY CUSTOMERS. YOU WANT ANOTHER BEER, BARN?
"O FOR A DRAUGHT OF VINTAGE! THAT HATH BEEN COOLED A LONG AGE IN THE DEEP DELVED EARTH."
HEY KID! YOU AIN'T ALLOWED IN HERE!
YES, OF COURSE, MY BEER MUST BE OF THE ROOT VARIETY, FOR I LIVE A LIFE OF UNMATCHED SOBRIETY. AND LONELINESS IS HOW I'LL GAIN MY NOTORIETY.
I AM TOUCHED THAT MY POEM, WHICH COMES FROM A PLACE OF SUCH PAIN, HAS INSPIRED EMOTION WITHIN YOU THAT HAS CAUSED YOU TO CRY.
HUH? OH, NO. I JUST CAUGHT A WHIFF OF BARNEY'S STINK, BUT YOU DID INSPIRE ME, KID. I GOT AN IDEA...

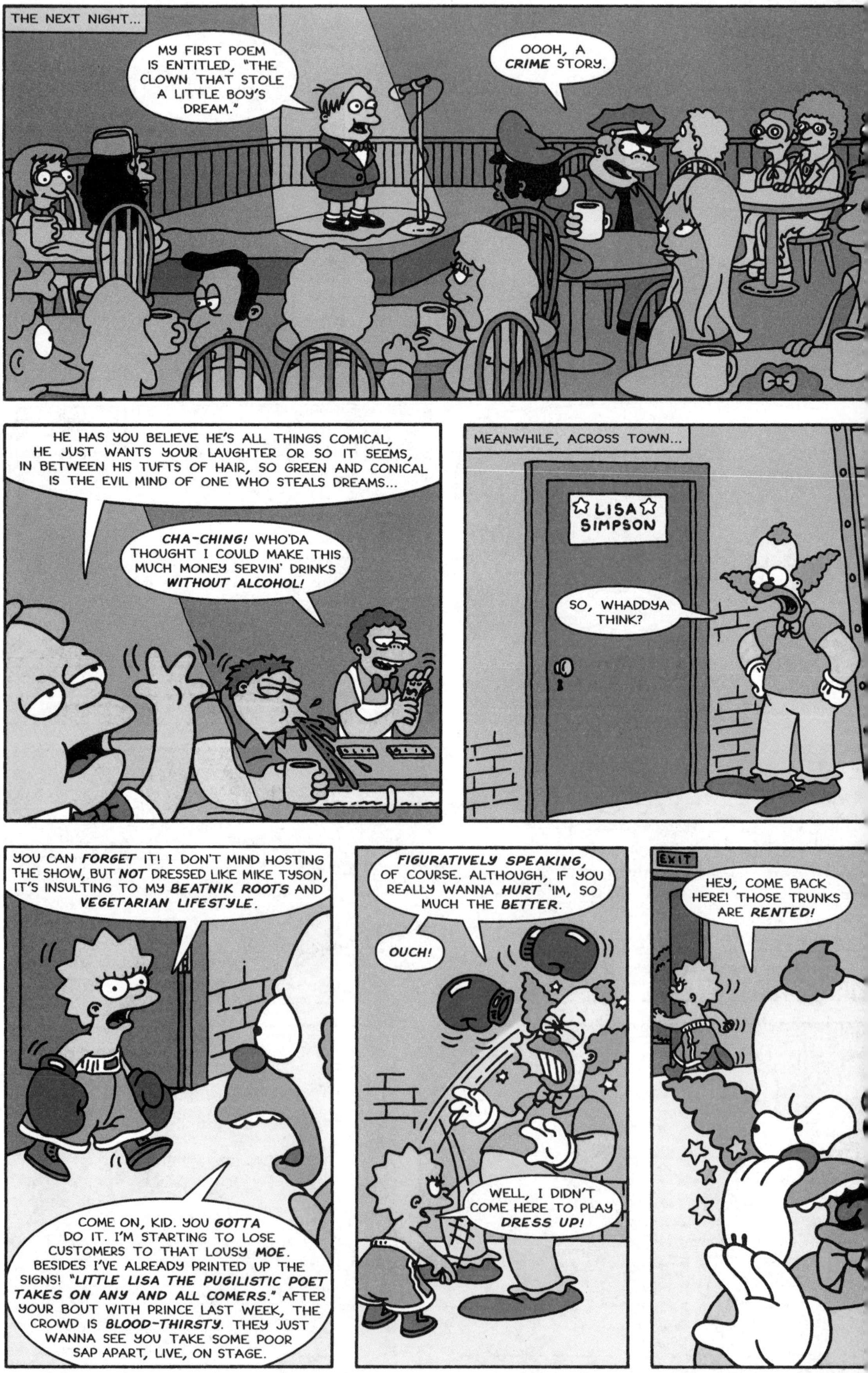
THE NEXT NIGHT...
MY FIRST POEM IS ENTITLED, "THE CLOWN THAT STOLE A LITTLE BOY'S DREAM."
OOOH, A CRIME STORY.
HE HAS YOU BELIEVE HE'S ALL THINGS COMICAL, HE JUST WANTS YOUR LAUGHTER OR SO IT SEEMS, IN BETWEEN HIS TUFTS OF HAIR, SO GREEN AND CONICAL IS THE EVIL MIND OF ONE WHO STEALS DREAMS...
CHA-CHING! WHO'DA THOUGHT I COULD MAKE THIS MUCH MONEY SERVIN' DRINKS WITHOUT ALCOHOL!
MEANWHILE, ACROSS TOWN...
LISA SIMPSON
SO, WHADDYA THINK?
YOU CAN FORGET IT! I DON'T MIND HOSTING THE SHOW, BUT NOT DRESSED LIKE MIKE TYSON, IT'S INSULTING TO MY BEATNIK ROOTS AND VEGETARIAN LIFESTYLE.
COME ON, KID. YOU GOTTA DO IT. I'M STARTING TO LOSE CUSTOMERS TO THAT LOUSY MOE. BESIDES I'VE ALREADY PRINTED UP THE SIGNS! "LITTLE LISA THE PUGILISTIC POET TAKES ON ANY AND ALL COMERS." AFTER YOUR BOUT WITH PRINCE LAST WEEK, THE CROWD IS BLOOD-THIRSTY. THEY JUST WANNA SEE YOU TAKE SOME POOR SAP APART, LIVE, ON STAGE.
FIGURATIVELY SPEAKING, OF COURSE. ALTHOUGH, IF YOU REALLY WANNA HURT 'IM, SO MUCH THE BETTER.
OUCH!
WELL, I DIDN'T COME HERE TO PLAY DRESS UP!
EXIT
HEY, COME BACK HERE! THOSE TRUNKS ARE RENTED!

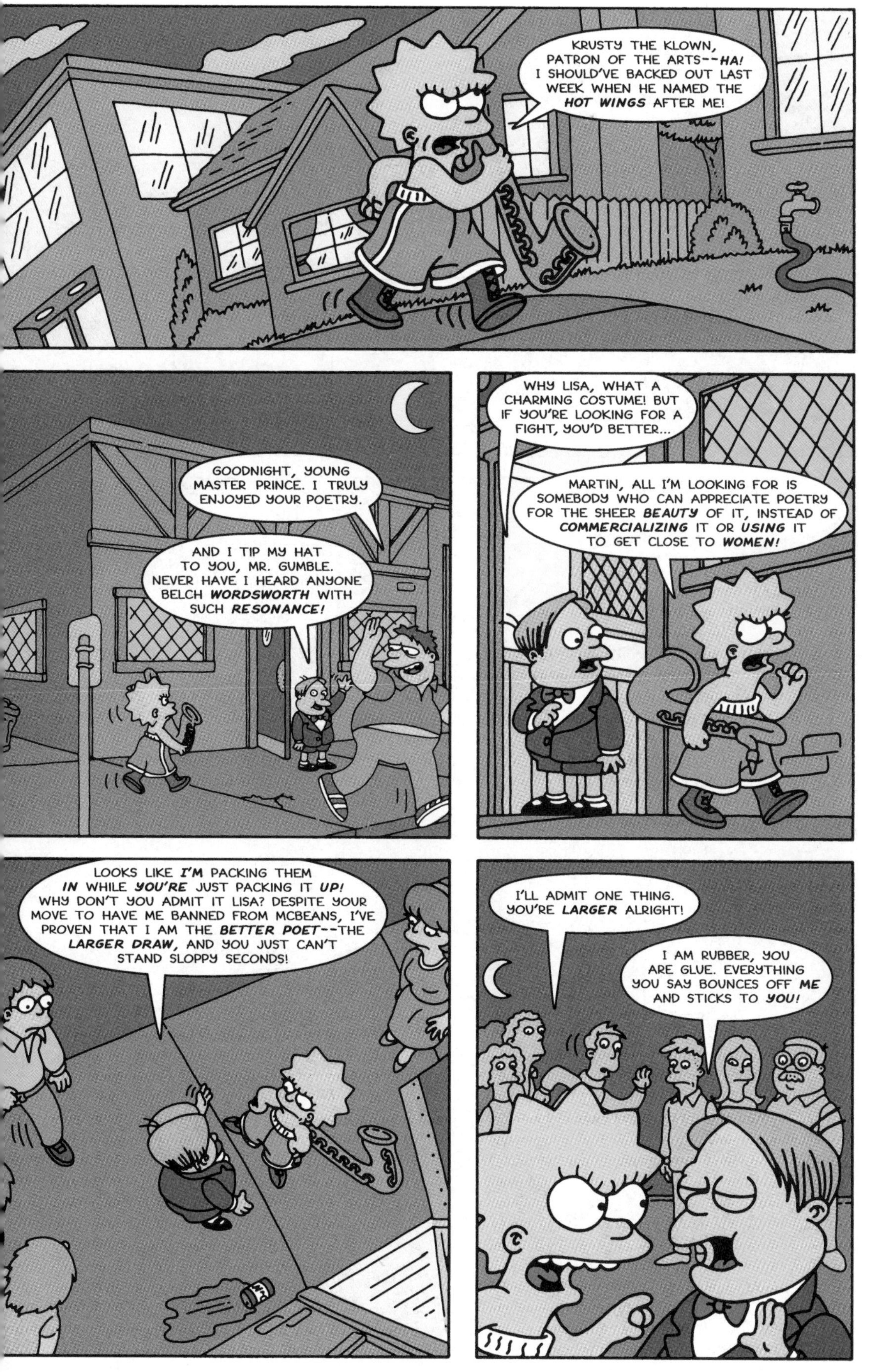
KRUSTY THE KLOWN, PATRON OF THE ARTS--HA! I SHOULD'VE BACKED OUT LAST WEEK WHEN HE NAMED THE HOT WINGS AFTER ME!
GOODNIGHT, YOUNG MASTER PRINCE. I TRULY ENJOYED YOUR POETRY.
AND I TIP MY HAT TO YOU, MR. GUMBLE. NEVER HAVE I HEARD ANYONE BELCH WORDSWORTH WITH SUCH RESONANCE!
WHY LISA, WHAT A CHARMING COSTUME! BUT IF YOU'RE LOOKING FOR A FIGHT, YOU'D BETTER...
MARTIN, ALL I'M LOOKING FOR IS SOMEBODY WHO CAN APPRECIATE POETRY FOR THE SHEER BEAUTY OF IT, INSTEAD OF COMMERCIALIZING IT OR USING IT TO GET CLOSE TO WOMEN!
LOOKS LIKE I'M PACKING THEM IN WHILE YOU'RE JUST PACKING IT UP! WHY DON'T YOU ADMIT IT LISA? DESPITE YOUR MOVE TO HAVE ME BANNED FROM MCBEANS, I'VE PROVEN THAT I AM THE BETTER POET--THE LARGER DRAW, AND YOU JUST CAN'T STAND SLOPPY SECONDS!
I'LL ADMIT ONE THING. YOU'RE LARGER ALRIGHT!
I AM RUBBER, YOU ARE GLUE. EVERYTHING YOU SAY BOUNCES OFF ME AND STICKS TO YOU!

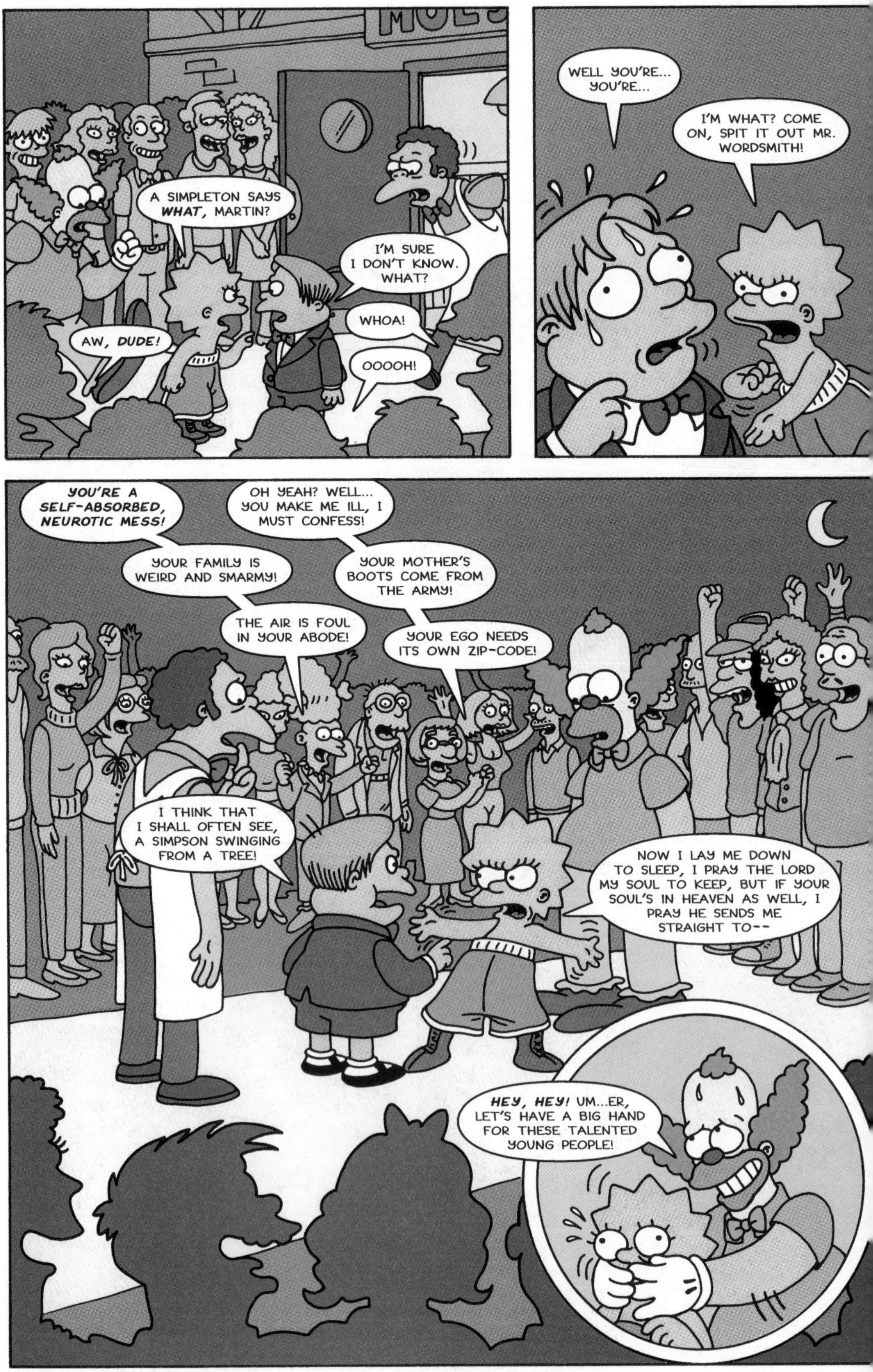

A SIMPLETON SAYS *WHAT,* MARTIN?
I'M SURE I DON'T KNOW. WHAT?
WHOA!
AW, *DUDE!*
OOOOH!
WELL YOU'RE... YOU'RE...
I'M WHAT? COME ON, SPIT IT OUT MR. WORDSMITH!
YOU'RE A SELF-ABSORBED, NEUROTIC MESS!
OH YEAH? WELL... YOU MAKE ME ILL, I MUST CONFESS!
YOUR FAMILY IS WEIRD AND SMARMY!
YOUR MOTHER'S BOOTS COME FROM THE ARMY!
THE AIR IS FOUL IN YOUR ABODE!
YOUR EGO NEEDS ITS OWN ZIP-CODE!
I THINK THAT I SHALL OFTEN SEE, A SIMPSON SWINGING FROM A TREE!
NOW I LAY ME DOWN TO SLEEP, I PRAY THE LORD MY SOUL TO KEEP, BUT IF YOUR SOUL'S IN HEAVEN AS WELL, I PRAY HE SENDS ME STRAIGHT TO--
HEY, HEY! UM...ER, LET'S HAVE A BIG HAND FOR THESE TALENTED YOUNG PEOPLE!

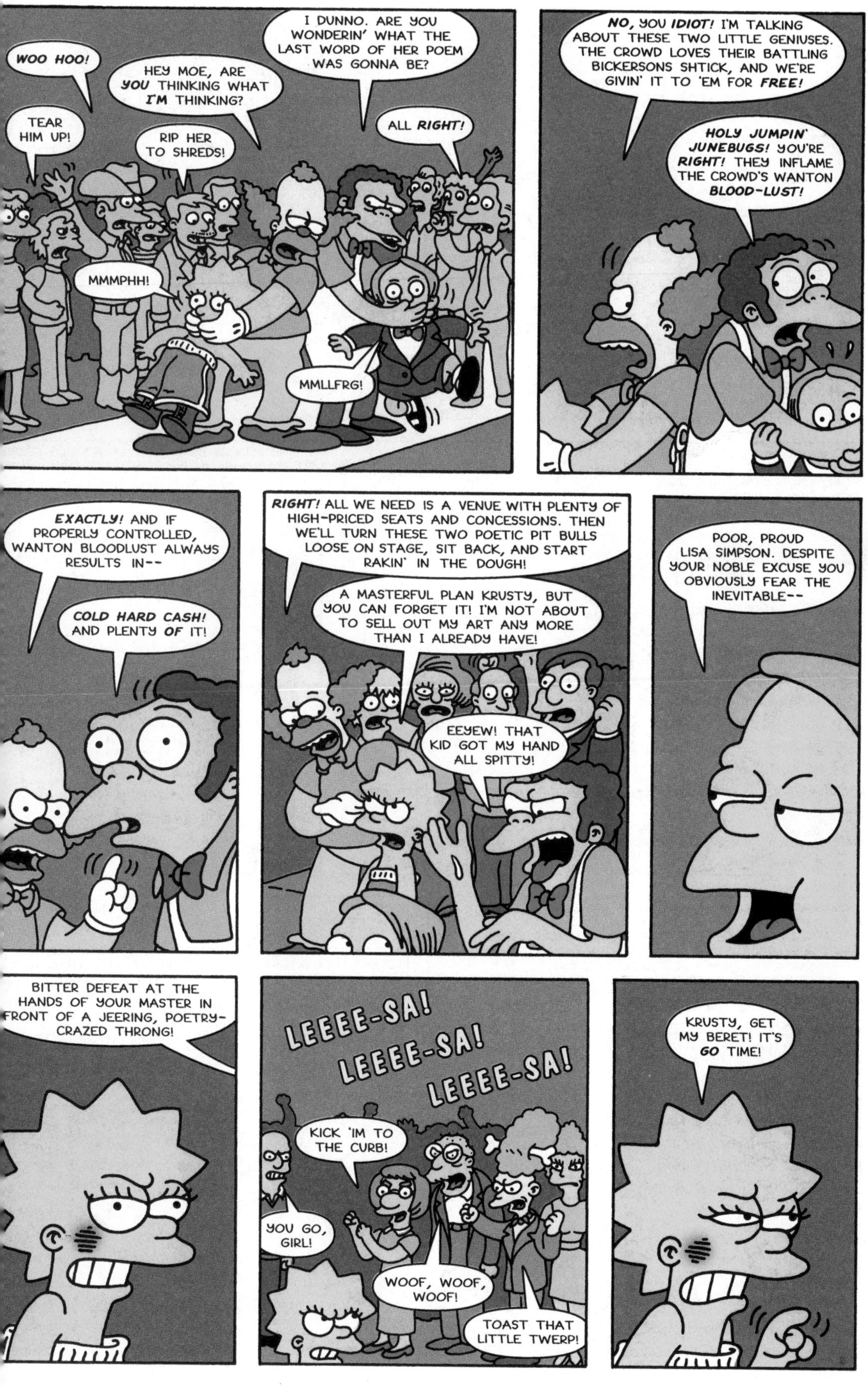
WOO HOO!
TEAR HIM UP!
HEY MOE, ARE YOU THINKING WHAT I'M THINKING?
RIP HER TO SHREDS!
I DUNNO. ARE YOU WONDERIN' WHAT THE LAST WORD OF HER POEM WAS GONNA BE?
ALL RIGHT!
MMMPHH!
MMLLFRG!
NO, YOU IDIOT! I'M TALKING ABOUT THESE TWO LITTLE GENIUSES. THE CROWD LOVES THEIR BATTLING BICKERSONS SHTICK, AND WE'RE GIVIN' IT TO 'EM FOR FREE!
HOLY JUMPIN' JUNEBUGS! YOU'RE RIGHT! THEY INFLAME THE CROWD'S WANTON BLOOD-LUST!
EXACTLY! AND IF PROPERLY CONTROLLED, WANTON BLOODLUST ALWAYS RESULTS IN--
COLD HARD CASH! AND PLENTY OF IT!
RIGHT! ALL WE NEED IS A VENUE WITH PLENTY OF HIGH-PRICED SEATS AND CONCESSIONS. THEN WE'LL TURN THESE TWO POETIC PIT BULLS LOOSE ON STAGE, SIT BACK, AND START RAKIN' IN THE DOUGH!
A MASTERFUL PLAN KRUSTY, BUT YOU CAN FORGET IT! I'M NOT ABOUT TO SELL OUT MY ART ANY MORE THAN I ALREADY HAVE!
EEYEW! THAT KID GOT MY HAND ALL SPITTY!
POOR, PROUD LISA SIMPSON. DESPITE YOUR NOBLE EXCUSE YOU OBVIOUSLY FEAR THE INEVITABLE--
BITTER DEFEAT AT THE HANDS OF YOUR MASTER IN FRONT OF A JEERING, POETRY-CRAZED THRONG!
LEEEE-SA!
LEEEE-SA!
LEEEE-SA!
KICK 'IM TO THE CURB!
YOU GO, GIRL!
WOOF, WOOF, WOOF!
TOAST THAT LITTLE TWERP!
KRUSTY, GET MY BERET! IT'S GO TIME!

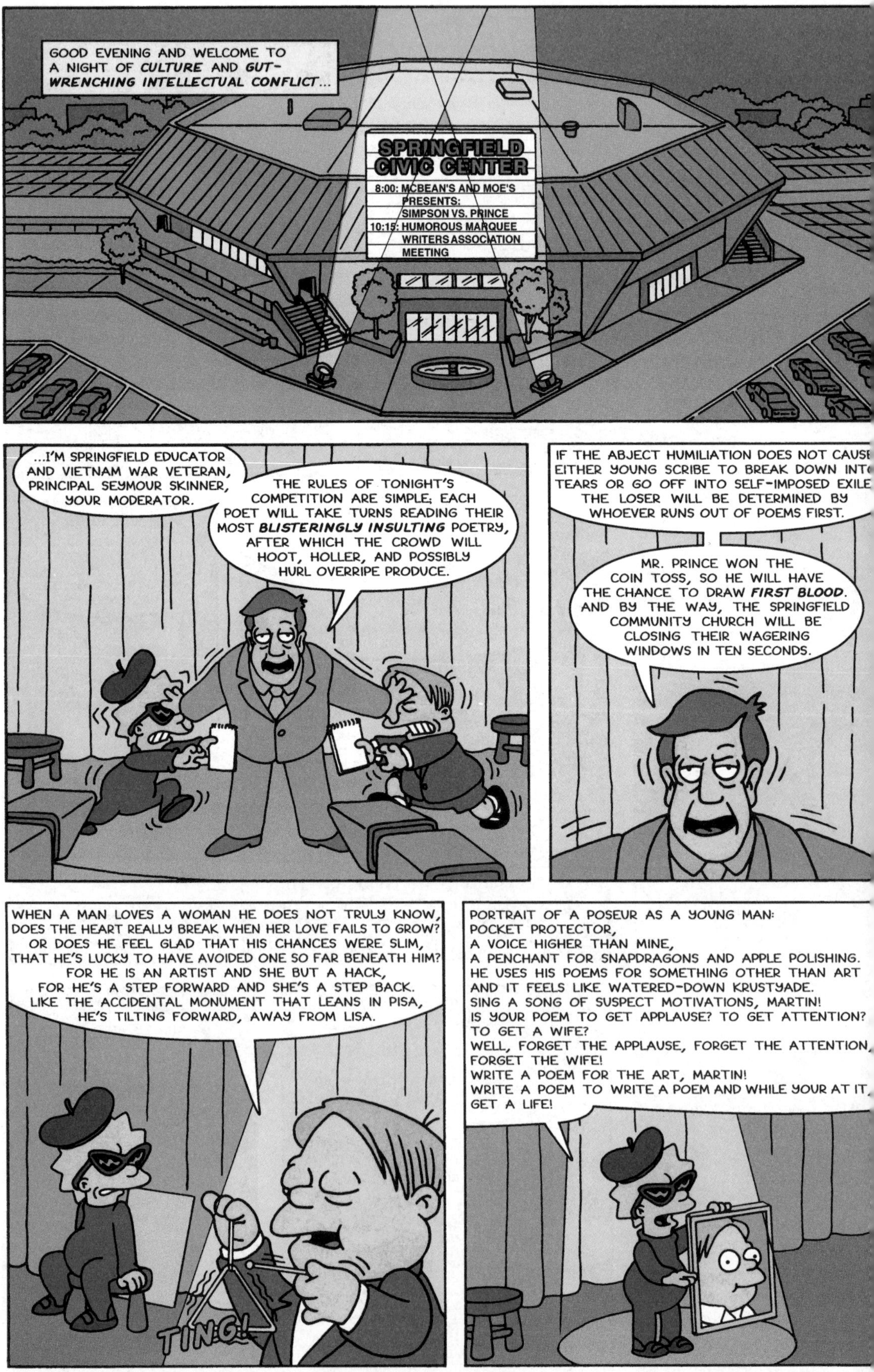

GOOD EVENING AND WELCOME TO A NIGHT OF *CULTURE* AND *GUT-WRENCHING INTELLECTUAL CONFLICT*...
SPRINGFIELD CIVIC CENTER
8:00: MCBEAN'S AND MOE'S PRESENTS: SIMPSON VS. PRINCE
10:15: HUMOROUS MARQUEE WRITERS ASSOCIATION MEETING
...I'M SPRINGFIELD EDUCATOR AND VIETNAM WAR VETERAN, PRINCIPAL SEYMOUR SKINNER, YOUR MODERATOR.
THE RULES OF TONIGHT'S COMPETITION ARE SIMPLE; EACH POET WILL TAKE TURNS READING THEIR MOST ***BLISTERINGLY INSULTING*** POETRY, AFTER WHICH THE CROWD WILL HOOT, HOLLER, AND POSSIBLY HURL OVERRIPE PRODUCE.
IF THE ABJECT HUMILIATION DOES NOT CAUS EITHER YOUNG SCRIBE TO BREAK DOWN INT TEARS OR GO OFF INTO SELF-IMPOSED EXILE THE LOSER WILL BE DETERMINED BY WHOEVER RUNS OUT OF POEMS FIRST.
MR. PRINCE WON THE COIN TOSS, SO HE WILL HAVE THE CHANCE TO DRAW ***FIRST BLOOD***. AND BY THE WAY, THE SPRINGFIELD COMMUNITY CHURCH WILL BE CLOSING THEIR WAGERING WINDOWS IN TEN SECONDS.
WHEN A MAN LOVES A WOMAN HE DOES NOT TRULY KNOW, DOES THE HEART REALLY BREAK WHEN HER LOVE FAILS TO GROW? OR DOES HE FEEL GLAD THAT HIS CHANCES WERE SLIM, THAT HE'S LUCKY TO HAVE AVOIDED ONE SO FAR BENEATH HIM? FOR HE IS AN ARTIST AND SHE BUT A HACK, FOR HE'S A STEP FORWARD AND SHE'S A STEP BACK. LIKE THE ACCIDENTAL MONUMENT THAT LEANS IN PISA, HE'S TILTING FORWARD, AWAY FROM LISA.
TING!
PORTRAIT OF A POSEUR AS A YOUNG MAN: POCKET PROTECTOR, A VOICE HIGHER THAN MINE, A PENCHANT FOR SNAPDRAGONS AND APPLE POLISHING. HE USES HIS POEMS FOR SOMETHING OTHER THAN ART AND IT FEELS LIKE WATERED-DOWN KRUSTYADE. SING A SONG OF SUSPECT MOTIVATIONS, MARTIN! IS YOUR POEM TO GET APPLAUSE? TO GET ATTENTION? TO GET A WIFE? WELL, FORGET THE APPLAUSE, FORGET THE ATTENTION, FORGET THE WIFE! WRITE A POEM FOR THE ART, MARTIN! WRITE A POEM TO WRITE A POEM AND WHILE YOUR AT IT, GET A LIFE!

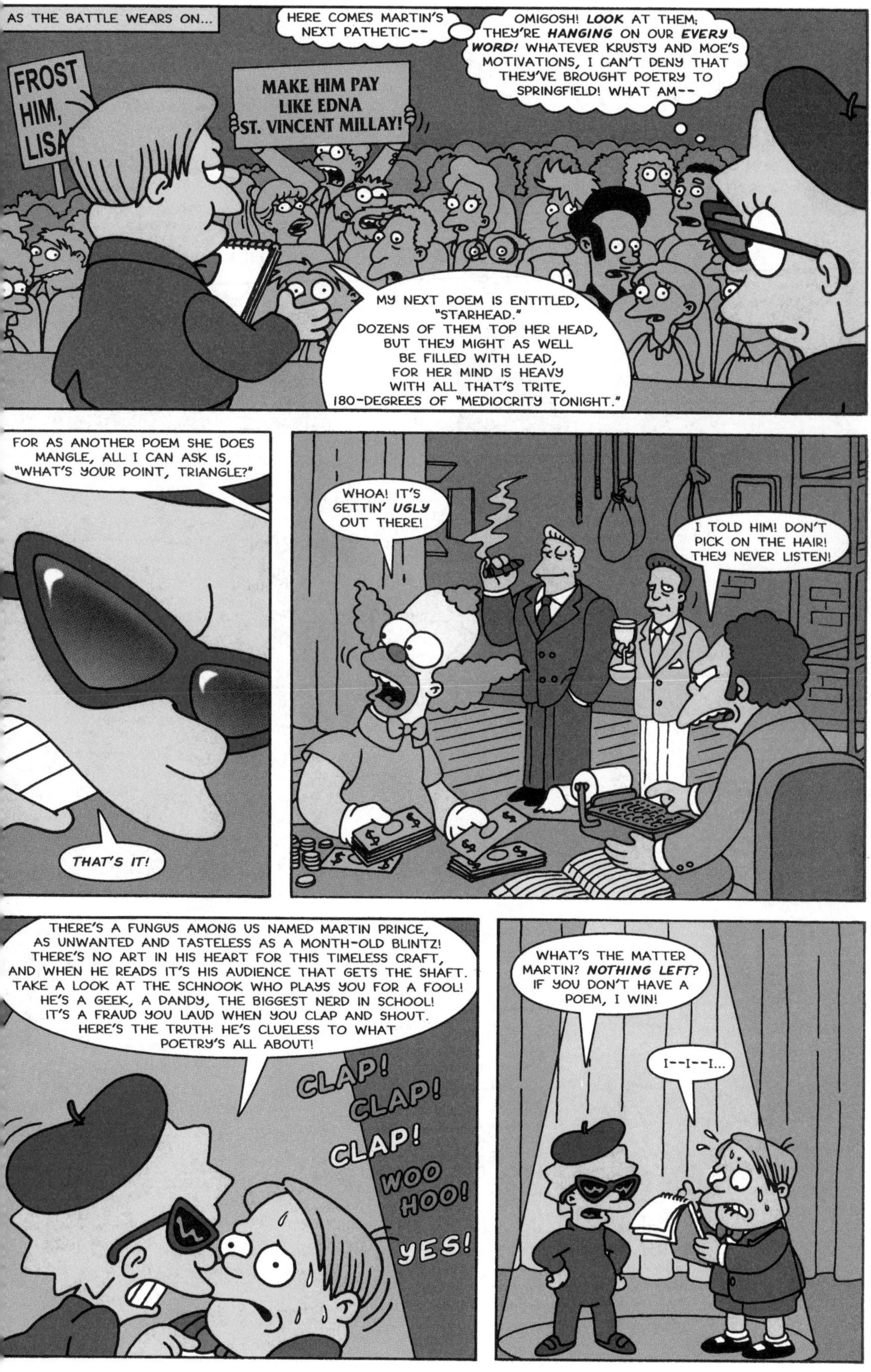
AS THE BATTLE WEARS ON...
FROST HIM, LISA
MAKE HIM PAY LIKE EDNA ST. VINCENT MILLAY!
HERE COMES MARTIN'S NEXT PATHETIC--
OMIGOSH! LOOK AT THEM; THEY'RE HANGING ON OUR EVERY WORD! WHATEVER KRUSTY AND MOE'S MOTIVATIONS, I CAN'T DENY THAT THEY'VE BROUGHT POETRY TO SPRINGFIELD! WHAT AM--
MY NEXT POEM IS ENTITLED, "STARHEAD." DOZENS OF THEM TOP HER HEAD, BUT THEY MIGHT AS WELL BE FILLED WITH LEAD, FOR HER MIND IS HEAVY WITH ALL THAT'S TRITE, 180-DEGREES OF "MEDIOCRITY TONIGHT."
FOR AS ANOTHER POEM SHE DOES MANGLE, ALL I CAN ASK IS, "WHAT'S YOUR POINT, TRIANGLE?"
THAT'S IT!
WHOA! IT'S GETTIN' UGLY OUT THERE!
I TOLD HIM! DON'T PICK ON THE HAIR! THEY NEVER LISTEN!
THERE'S A FUNGUS AMONG US NAMED MARTIN PRINCE, AS UNWANTED AND TASTELESS AS A MONTH-OLD BLINTZ! THERE'S NO ART IN HIS HEART FOR THIS TIMELESS CRAFT, AND WHEN HE READS IT'S HIS AUDIENCE THAT GETS THE SHAFT. TAKE A LOOK AT THE SCHNOOK WHO PLAYS YOU FOR A FOOL! HE'S A GEEK, A DANDY, THE BIGGEST NERD IN SCHOOL! IT'S A FRAUD YOU LAUD WHEN YOU CLAP AND SHOUT. HERE'S THE TRUTH: HE'S CLUELESS TO WHAT POETRY'S ALL ABOUT!
CLAP! CLAP! CLAP! WOO HOO! YES!
WHAT'S THE MATTER MARTIN? NOTHING LEFT? IF YOU DON'T HAVE A POEM, I WIN!
I--I--I...

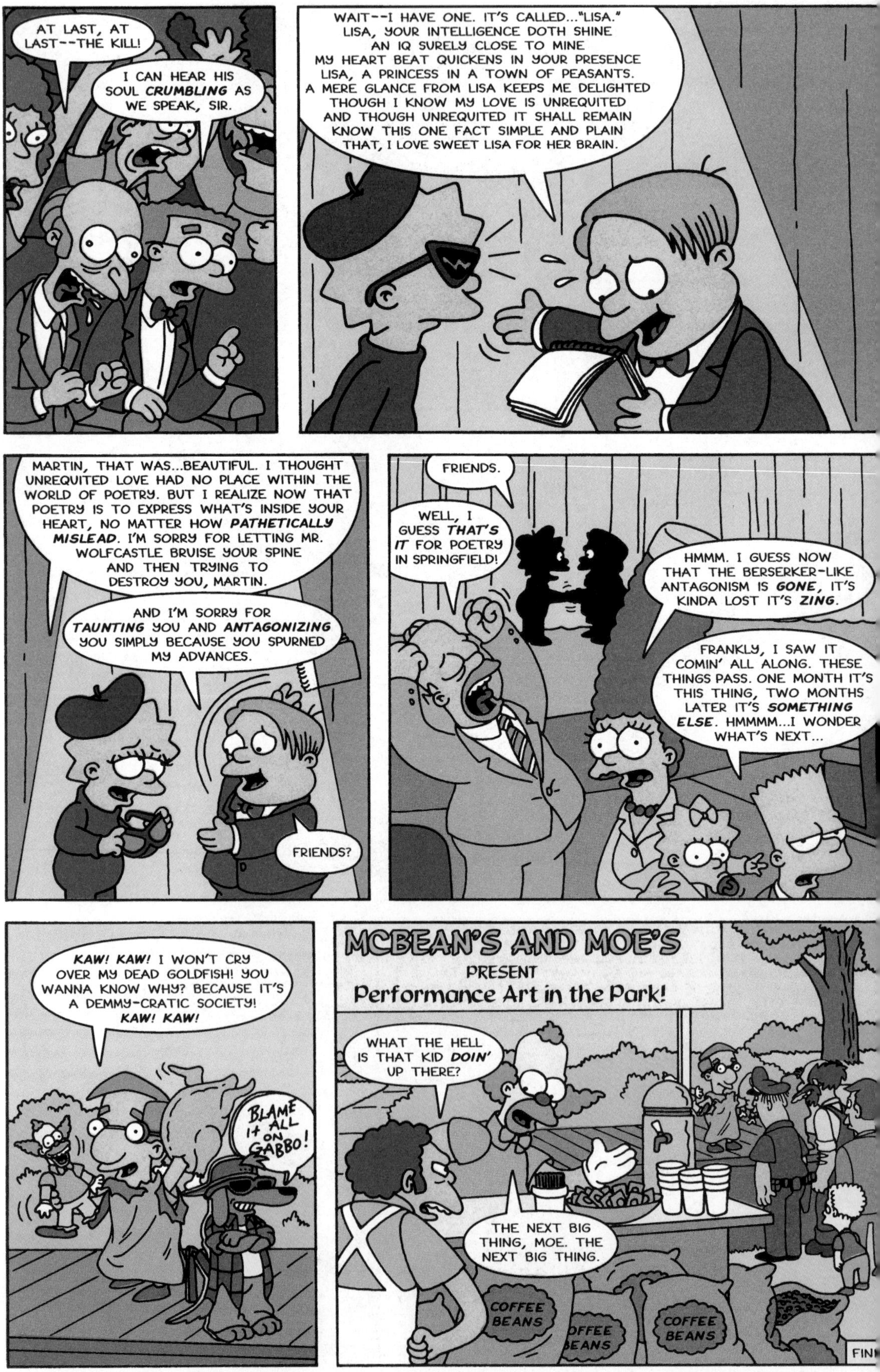
AT LAST, AT LAST--THE KILL!
I CAN HEAR HIS SOUL CRUMBLING AS WE SPEAK, SIR.
WAIT--I HAVE ONE. IT'S CALLED..."LISA." LISA, YOUR INTELLIGENCE DOTH SHINE AN IQ SURELY CLOSE TO MINE MY HEART BEAT QUICKENS IN YOUR PRESENCE LISA, A PRINCESS IN A TOWN OF PEASANTS. A MERE GLANCE FROM LISA KEEPS ME DELIGHTED THOUGH I KNOW MY LOVE IS UNREQUITED AND THOUGH UNREQUITED IT SHALL REMAIN KNOW THIS ONE FACT SIMPLE AND PLAIN THAT, I LOVE SWEET LISA FOR HER BRAIN.
MARTIN, THAT WAS...BEAUTIFUL. I THOUGHT UNREQUITED LOVE HAD NO PLACE WITHIN THE WORLD OF POETRY. BUT I REALIZE NOW THAT POETRY IS TO EXPRESS WHAT'S INSIDE YOUR HEART, NO MATTER HOW PATHETICALLY MISLEAD. I'M SORRY FOR LETTING MR. WOLFCASTLE BRUISE YOUR SPINE AND THEN TRYING TO DESTROY YOU, MARTIN.
AND I'M SORRY FOR TAUNTING YOU AND ANTAGONIZING YOU SIMPLY BECAUSE YOU SPURNED MY ADVANCES.
FRIENDS?
FRIENDS.
WELL, I GUESS THAT'S IT FOR POETRY IN SPRINGFIELD!
HMMM. I GUESS NOW THAT THE BERSERKER-LIKE ANTAGONISM IS GONE, IT'S KINDA LOST IT'S ZING.
FRANKLY, I SAW IT COMIN' ALL ALONG. THESE THINGS PASS. ONE MONTH IT'S THIS THING, TWO MONTHS LATER IT'S SOMETHING ELSE. HMMMM...I WONDER WHAT'S NEXT...
KAW! KAW! I WON'T CRY OVER MY DEAD GOLDFISH! YOU WANNA KNOW WHY? BECAUSE IT'S A DEMMY-CRATIC SOCIETY! KAW! KAW!
BLAME it ALL ON GABBO!
MCBEAN'S AND MOE'S PRESENT Performance Art in the Park!
WHAT THE HELL IS THAT KID DOIN' UP THERE?
THE NEXT BIG THING, MOE. THE NEXT BIG THING.
COFFEE BEANS
OFFEE BEANS
COFFEE BEANS
FIN

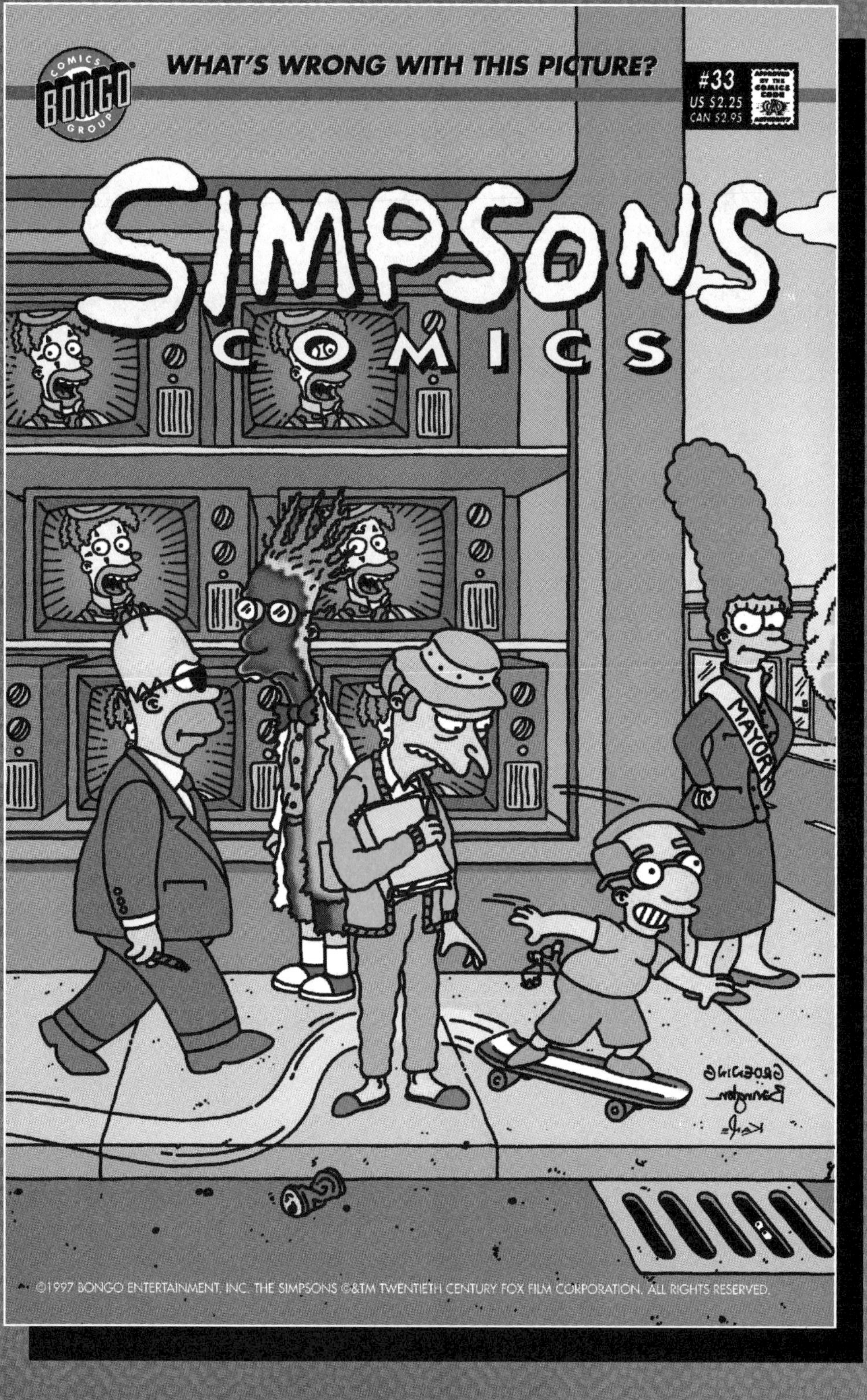

BONGO COMICS GROUP
WHAT'S WRONG WITH THIS PICTURE?
#33
US $2.25
CAN $2.95
SIMPSONS
COMICS
MAYOR
©1997 BONGO ENTERTAINMENT, INC. THE SIMPSONS ©&TM TWENTIETH CENTURY FOX FILM CORPORATION. ALL RIGHTS RESERVED.

Principal Skinner's Bottom 40

40. The first day of yet another school year
39. Wretched, ungrateful students who fail to appreciate the priceless gift we educators are trying to bestow upon them
38. Hooliganism
37. Having to actually eat in the cafeteria occasionally, to keep up appearances
36. Students who don't clean their plates
35. Recurrent screaming nightmares that I am a grade school principal
34. The way Groundskeeper Willie always fertilizes whichever section of the school grounds is upwind from my office window
33. "Talent" Night
32. The way the sound of a cherry-bombed toilet sets off my Vietnam flashbacks
31. Food fights
30. The smell of the teachers' lounge
29. When a trusted hall monitor goes bad
28. Whoever is drinking out of the flask I keep in my bottom drawer
27. Unflattering caricatures of me spraypainted on school walls
26. Namby-pamby school board members who won't allow kids to be spanked like in the good old days
25. The ongoing failure of the Springfield School Board to name me "Principal of the Year"
24. Teachers who lack the gumption to flunk their entire class
23. Water balloons
22. Comic books
21. Slingshots
20. Stink bombs
19. Mayhem
18. Kids who won't snitch on their friends
17. The embarrassment of yet another 0-14 season for our Junior Pumas soccer team
16. Having to change my unlisted home pho number 21 times in the last year—and still they call
15. Whoever started the vicious rumor tha wear a toupee
14. Disorder
13. Whoever keeps writing, "I AM A WIENER" in the dirt on my car's back window
12. Parent-teacher meetings
11. Faculty meetings
10. Uppity teachers who think they are more important to this institution than I am
9. The fact that the kids have learned my childhood nickname "Spanky"
8. Seeing former students go on to achieve great success in the outside world—fortunately, very few of them have
7. Boom boxes
6. T-shirts with slogans that encourage disrespect for authority
5. Snotty little punks who laugh at me beh my back
4. Knowing I have to endure another 17 years of this living hell before I can ta early retirement
3. Underachievers who are proud of it
2. Bart Simpson
1. El Barto—whoever you are, I vow that someday I will make you pay!

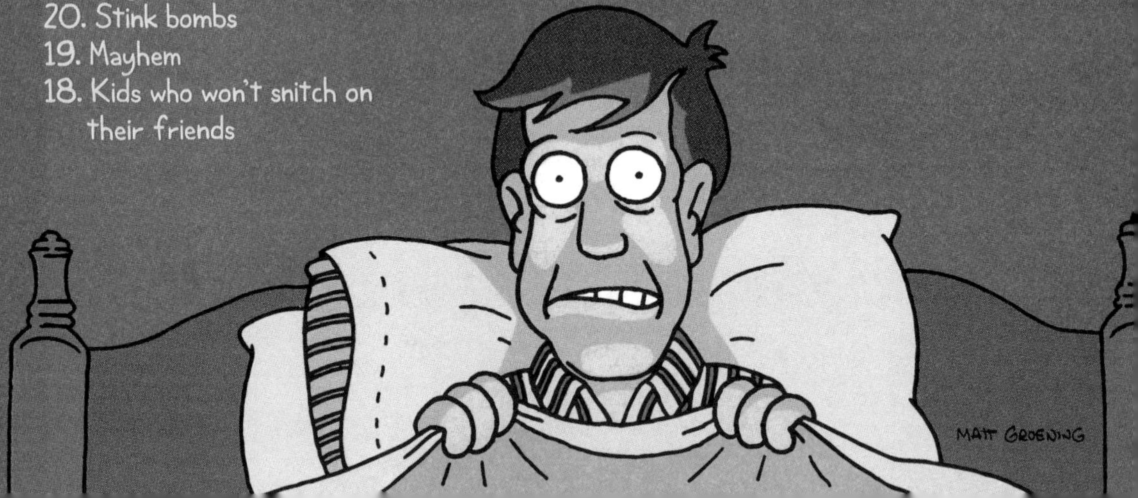
MATT GROENING

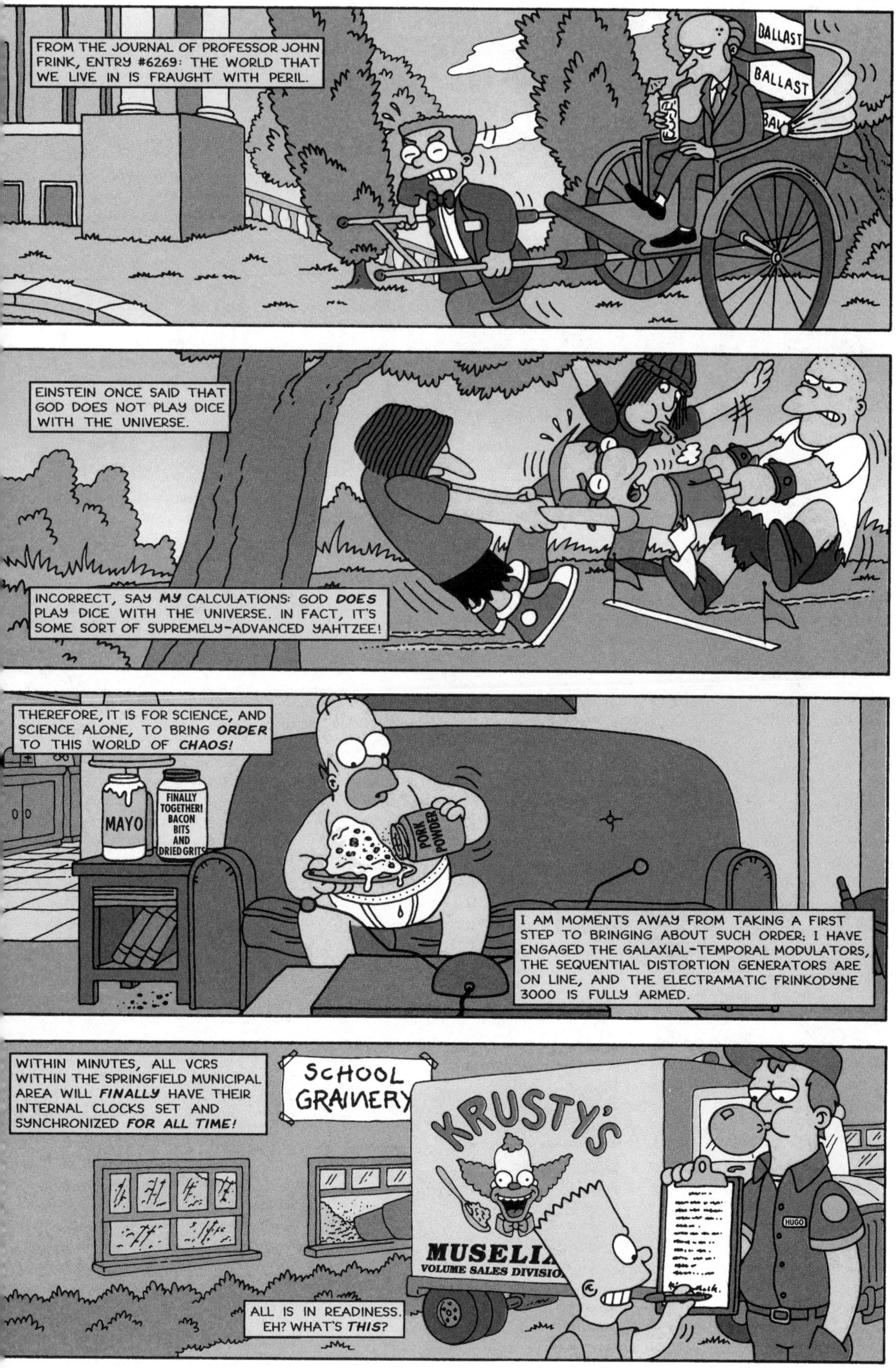

FROM THE JOURNAL OF PROFESSOR JOHN FRINK, ENTRY #6269: THE WORLD THAT WE LIVE IN IS FRAUGHT WITH PERIL.
BALLAST
BALLAST
EINSTEIN ONCE SAID THAT GOD DOES NOT PLAY DICE WITH THE UNIVERSE.
INCORRECT, SAY *MY* CALCULATIONS: GOD *DOES* PLAY DICE WITH THE UNIVERSE. IN FACT, IT'S SOME SORT OF SUPREMELY-ADVANCED YAHTZEE!
THEREFORE, IT IS FOR SCIENCE, AND SCIENCE ALONE, TO BRING *ORDER* TO THIS WORLD OF *CHAOS!*
MAYO
FINALLY TOGETHER! BACON BITS AND DRIED GRITS
PORK POWDER
I AM MOMENTS AWAY FROM TAKING A FIRST STEP TO BRINGING ABOUT SUCH ORDER; I HAVE ENGAGED THE GALAXIAL-TEMPORAL MODULATORS, THE SEQUENTIAL DISTORTION GENERATORS ARE ON LINE, AND THE ELECTRAMATIC FRINKODYNE 3000 IS FULLY ARMED.
WITHIN MINUTES, ALL VCRS WITHIN THE SPRINGFIELD MUNICIPAL AREA WILL *FINALLY* HAVE THEIR INTERNAL CLOCKS SET AND SYNCHRONIZED *FOR ALL TIME!*
SCHOOL GRAINERY
KRUSTY'S
MUSELIA
VOLUME SALES DIVISIO
HUGO
ALL IS IN READINESS. EH? WHAT'S *THIS*?

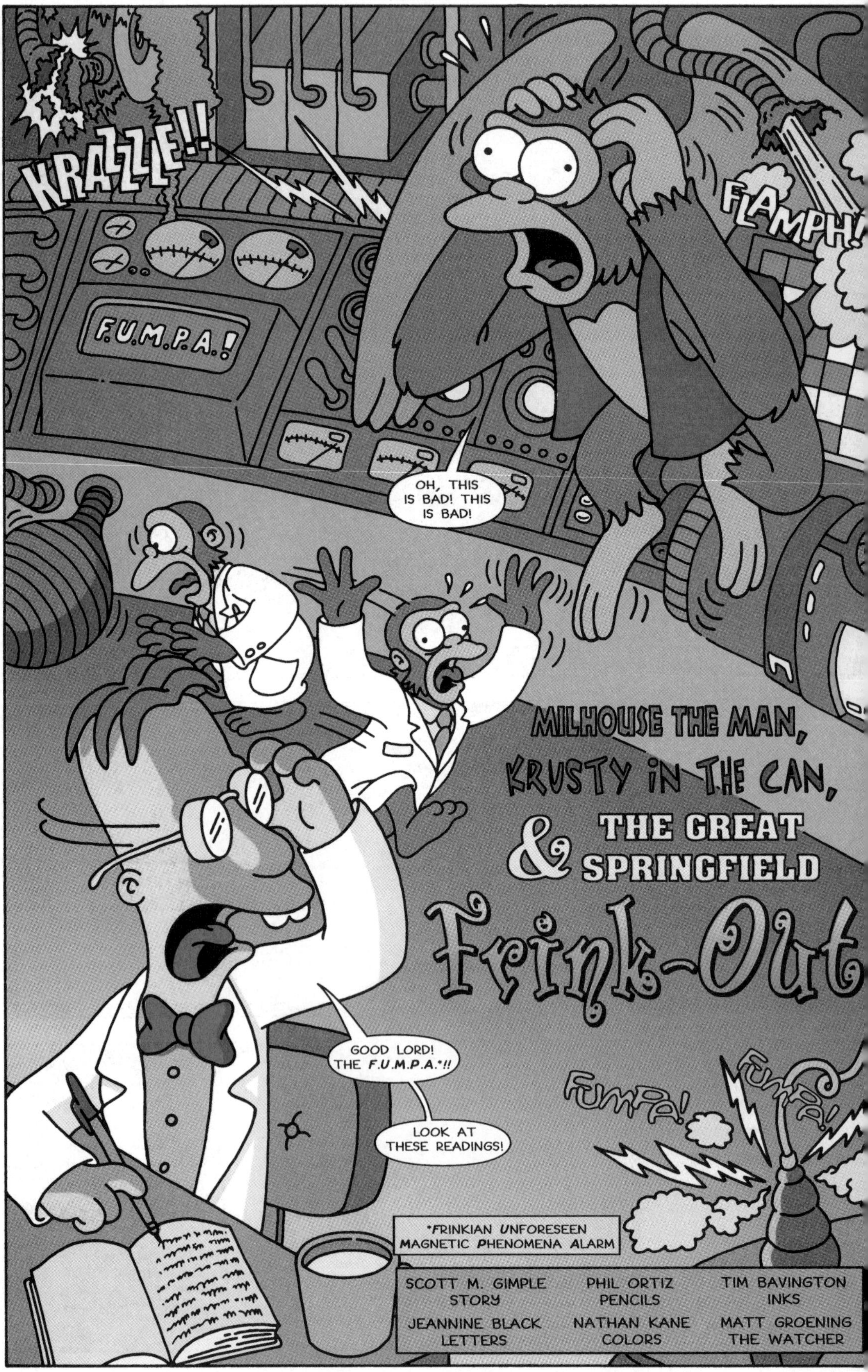
KRAZZLE!!
F.U.M.P.A.!
FLAMPH!
OH, THIS IS BAD! THIS IS BAD!
MILHOUSE THE MAN, KRUSTY IN THE CAN, & THE GREAT SPRINGFIELD Frink-Out
GOOD LORD! THE F.U.M.P.A.*!!
LOOK AT THESE READINGS!
FUMPA!
FUMPA!
*FRINKIAN UNFORESEEN MAGNETIC PHENOMENA ALARM
SCOTT M. GIMPLE STORY
PHIL ORTIZ PENCILS
TIM BAVINGTON INKS
JEANNINE BLACK LETTERS
NATHAN KANE COLORS
MATT GROENING THE WATCHER

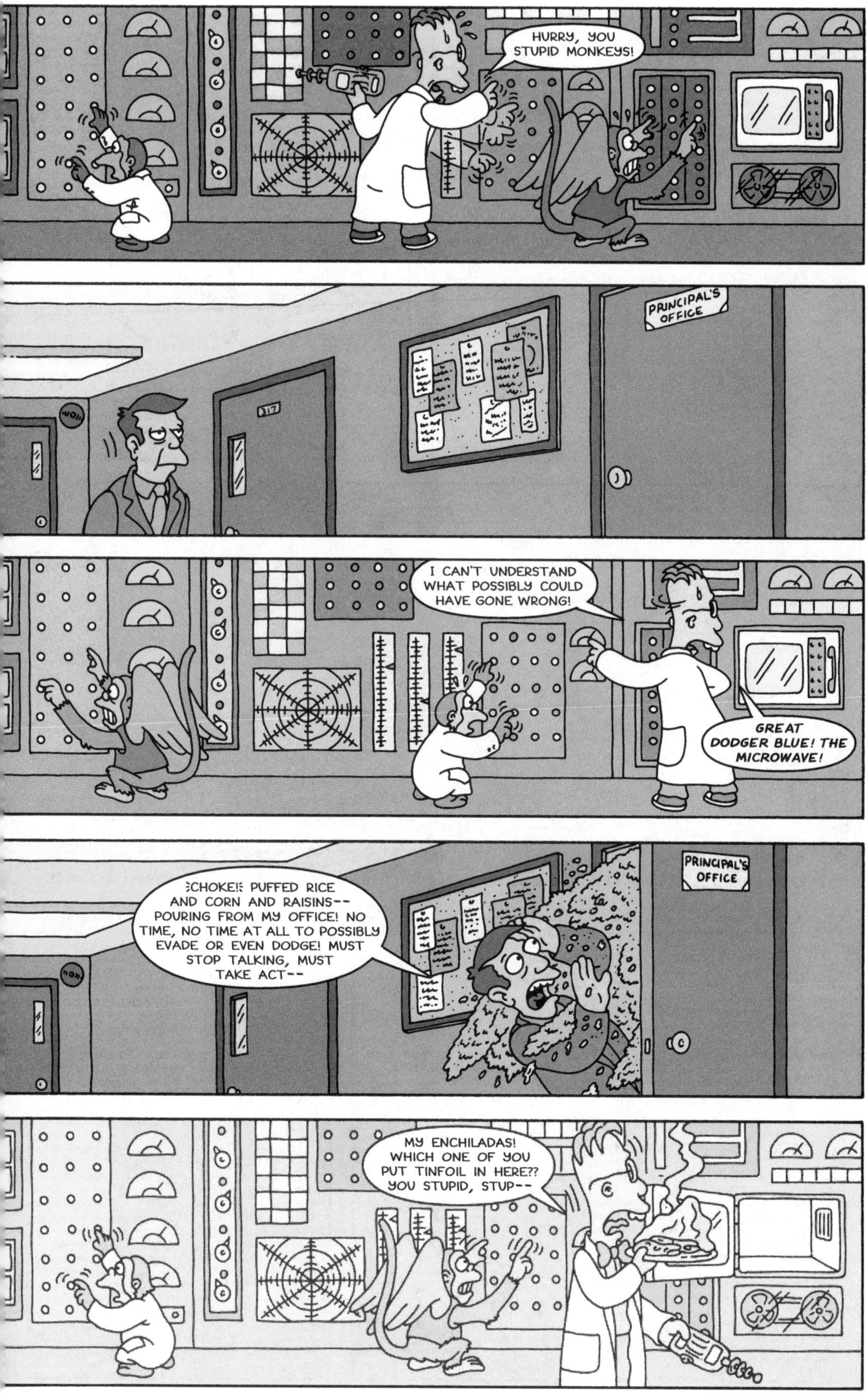
HURRY, YOU STUPID MONKEYS!
PRINCIPAL'S OFFICE
317
I CAN'T UNDERSTAND WHAT POSSIBLY COULD HAVE GONE WRONG!
GREAT DODGER BLUE! THE MICROWAVE!
PRINCIPAL'S OFFICE
⁝CHOKE!⁝ PUFFED RICE AND CORN AND RAISINS-- POURING FROM MY OFFICE! NO TIME, NO TIME AT ALL TO POSSIBLY EVADE OR EVEN DODGE! MUST STOP TALKING, MUST TAKE ACT--
MY ENCHILADAS! WHICH ONE OF YOU PUT TINFOIL IN HERE?? YOU STUPID, STUP--

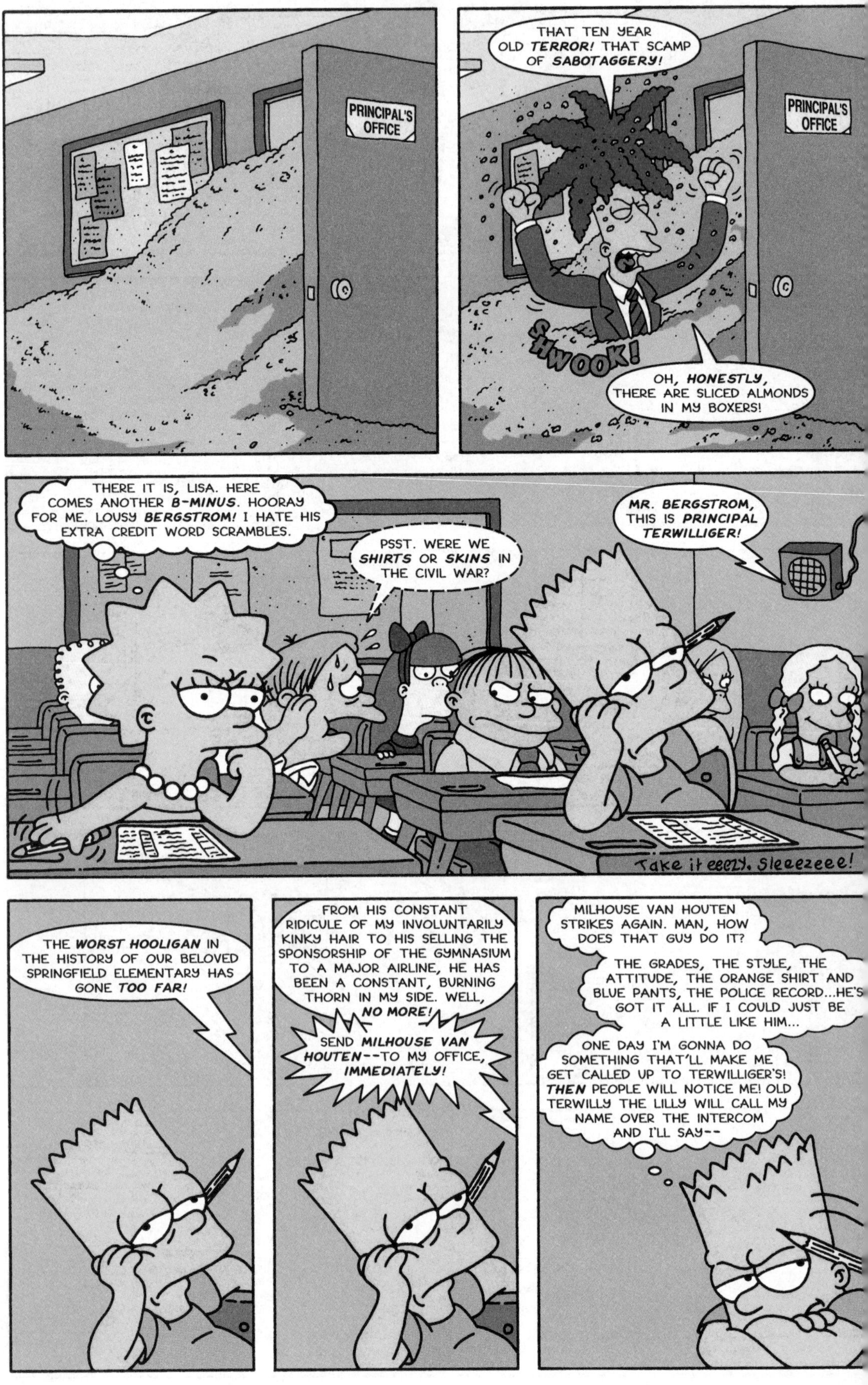
PRINCIPAL'S OFFICE
THAT TEN YEAR OLD TERROR! THAT SCAMP OF SABOTAGGERY!
PRINCIPAL'S OFFICE
SHWOOK!
OH, HONESTLY, THERE ARE SLICED ALMONDS IN MY BOXERS!
THERE IT IS, LISA. HERE COMES ANOTHER B-MINUS. HOORAY FOR ME. LOUSY BERGSTROM! I HATE HIS EXTRA CREDIT WORD SCRAMBLES.
PSST. WERE WE SHIRTS OR SKINS IN THE CIVIL WAR?
MR. BERGSTROM, THIS IS PRINCIPAL TERWILLIGER!
Take it eeezy, Sleeezeee!
THE WORST HOOLIGAN IN THE HISTORY OF OUR BELOVED SPRINGFIELD ELEMENTARY HAS GONE TOO FAR!
FROM HIS CONSTANT RIDICULE OF MY INVOLUNTARILY KINKY HAIR TO HIS SELLING THE SPONSORSHIP OF THE GYMNASIUM TO A MAJOR AIRLINE, HE HAS BEEN A CONSTANT, BURNING THORN IN MY SIDE. WELL, NO MORE!
SEND MILHOUSE VAN HOUTEN--TO MY OFFICE, IMMEDIATELY!
MILHOUSE VAN HOUTEN STRIKES AGAIN. MAN, HOW DOES THAT GUY DO IT?
THE GRADES, THE STYLE, THE ATTITUDE, THE ORANGE SHIRT AND BLUE PANTS, THE POLICE RECORD...HE'S GOT IT ALL. IF I COULD JUST BE A LITTLE LIKE HIM...
ONE DAY I'M GONNA DO SOMETHING THAT'LL MAKE ME GET CALLED UP TO TERWILLIGER'S! THEN PEOPLE WILL NOTICE ME! OLD TERWILLY THE LILLY WILL CALL MY NAME OVER THE INTERCOM AND I'LL SAY--

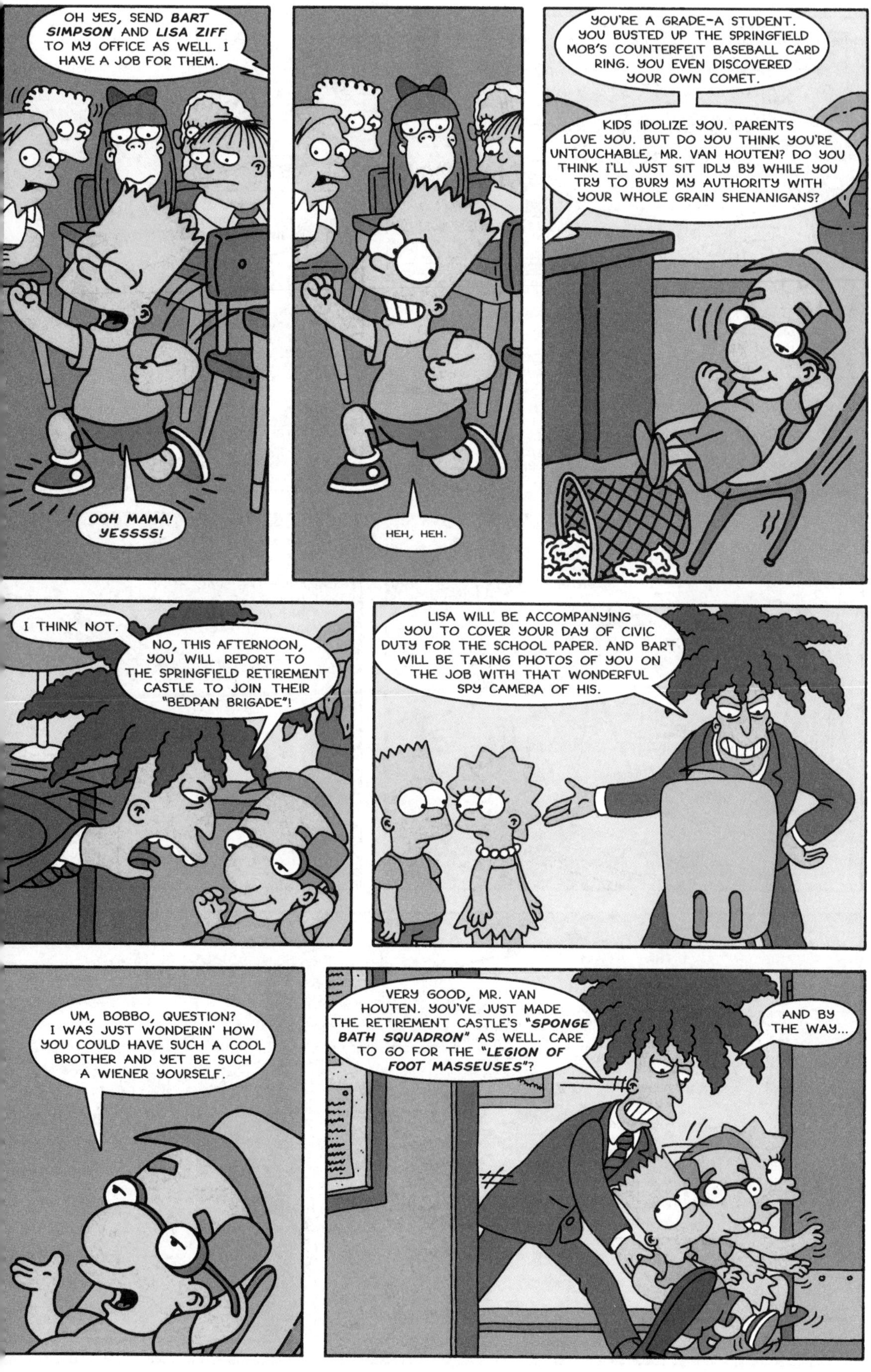
OH YES, SEND **BART SIMPSON** AND **LISA ZIFF** TO MY OFFICE AS WELL. I HAVE A JOB FOR THEM.
OOH MAMA! YESSSS!
HEH, HEH.
YOU'RE A GRADE-A STUDENT. YOU BUSTED UP THE SPRINGFIELD MOB'S COUNTERFEIT BASEBALL CARD RING. YOU EVEN DISCOVERED YOUR OWN COMET.
KIDS IDOLIZE YOU. PARENTS LOVE YOU. BUT DO YOU THINK YOU'RE UNTOUCHABLE, MR. VAN HOUTEN? DO YOU THINK I'LL JUST SIT IDLY BY WHILE YOU TRY TO BURY MY AUTHORITY WITH YOUR WHOLE GRAIN SHENANIGANS?
I THINK NOT.
NO, THIS AFTERNOON, YOU WILL REPORT TO THE SPRINGFIELD RETIREMENT CASTLE TO JOIN THEIR "BEDPAN BRIGADE"!
LISA WILL BE ACCOMPANYING YOU TO COVER YOUR DAY OF CIVIC DUTY FOR THE SCHOOL PAPER. AND BART WILL BE TAKING PHOTOS OF YOU ON THE JOB WITH THAT WONDERFUL SPY CAMERA OF HIS.
UM, BOBBO, QUESTION? I WAS JUST WONDERIN' HOW YOU COULD HAVE SUCH A COOL BROTHER AND YET BE SUCH A WIENER YOURSELF.
VERY GOOD, MR. VAN HOUTEN. YOU'VE JUST MADE THE RETIREMENT CASTLE'S ***"SPONGE BATH SQUADRON"*** AS WELL. CARE TO GO FOR THE ***"LEGION OF FOOT MASSEUSES"***?
AND BY THE WAY...

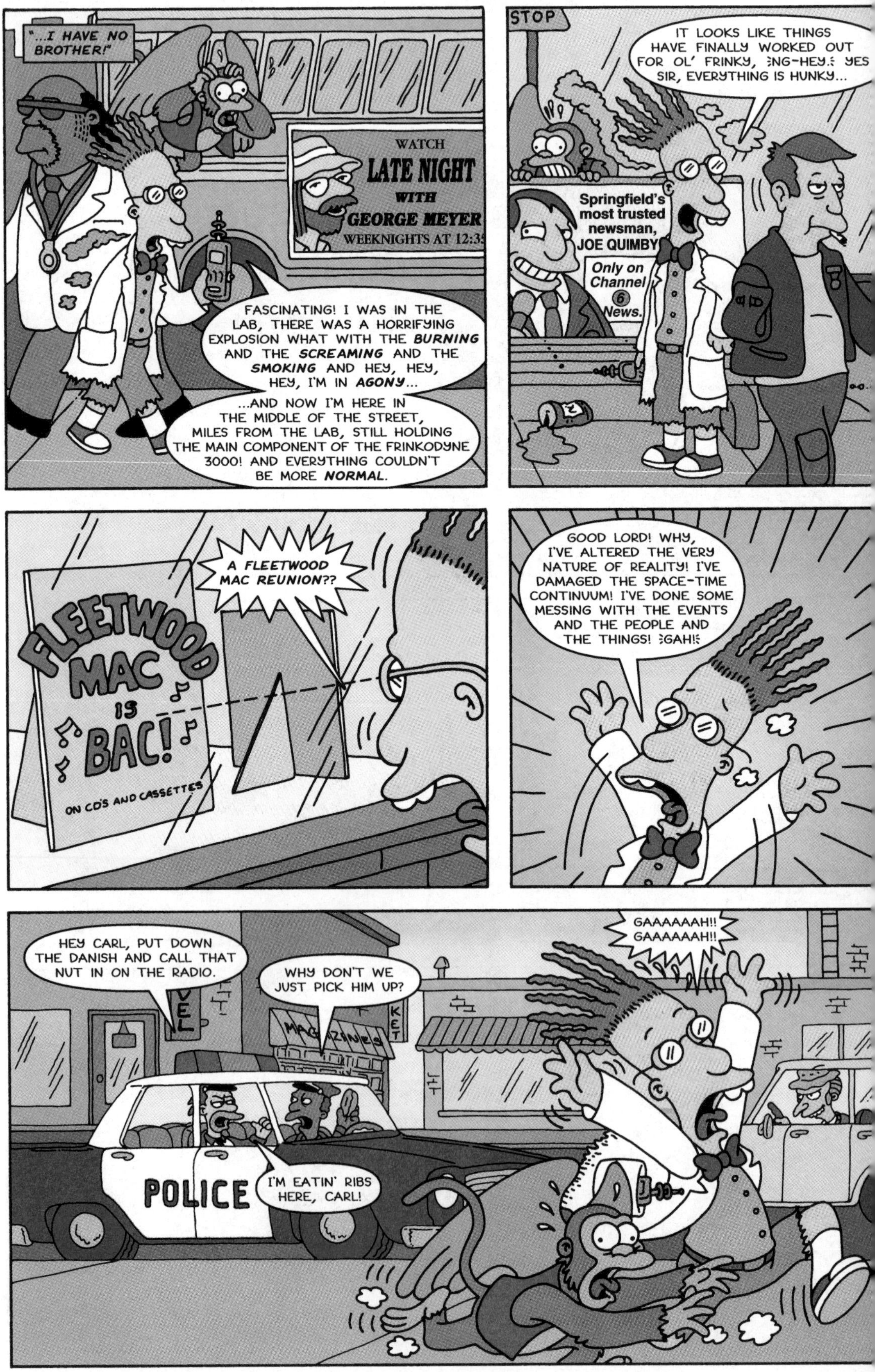
"...I HAVE NO BROTHER!"
WATCH LATE NIGHT WITH GEORGE MEYER WEEKNIGHTS AT 12:35
FASCINATING! I WAS IN THE LAB, THERE WAS A HORRIFYING EXPLOSION WHAT WITH THE *BURNING* AND THE *SCREAMING* AND THE *SMOKING* AND HEY, HEY, HEY, I'M IN *AGONY*...
...AND NOW I'M HERE IN THE MIDDLE OF THE STREET, MILES FROM THE LAB, STILL HOLDING THE MAIN COMPONENT OF THE FRINKODYNE 3000! AND EVERYTHING COULDN'T BE MORE *NORMAL*.
STOP
IT LOOKS LIKE THINGS HAVE FINALLY WORKED OUT FOR OL' FRINKY, ꞮNG-HEY.Ꞽ YES SIR, EVERYTHING IS HUNKY...
Springfield's most trusted newsman, JOE QUIMBY
Only on Channel 6 News.
A *FLEETWOOD MAC REUNION*??
FLEETWOOD MAC IS BAC!
ON CD'S AND CASSETTES
GOOD LORD! WHY, I'VE ALTERED THE VERY NATURE OF REALITY! I'VE DAMAGED THE SPACE-TIME CONTINUUM! I'VE DONE SOME MESSING WITH THE EVENTS AND THE PEOPLE AND THE THINGS! ꞮGAH!Ꞽ
HEY CARL, PUT DOWN THE DANISH AND CALL THAT NUT IN ON THE RADIO.
WHY DON'T WE JUST PICK HIM UP?
I'M EATIN' RIBS HERE, CARL!
GAAAAAAH!! GAAAAAAH!!
POLICE
MAGAZINES

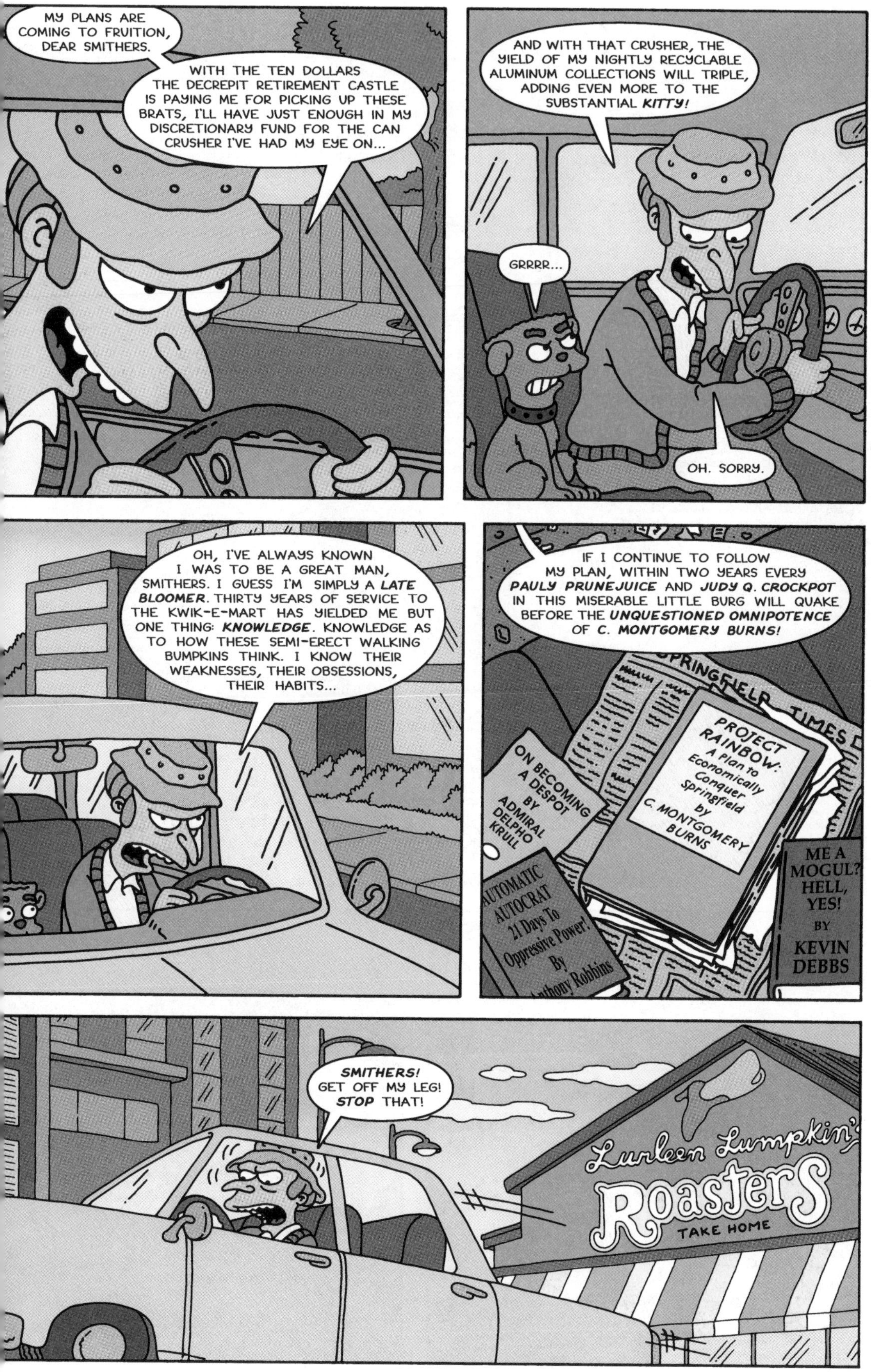
MY PLANS ARE COMING TO FRUITION, DEAR SMITHERS.
WITH THE TEN DOLLARS THE DECREPIT RETIREMENT CASTLE IS PAYING ME FOR PICKING UP THESE BRATS, I'LL HAVE JUST ENOUGH IN MY DISCRETIONARY FUND FOR THE CAN CRUSHER I'VE HAD MY EYE ON...
AND WITH THAT CRUSHER, THE YIELD OF MY NIGHTLY RECYCLABLE ALUMINUM COLLECTIONS WILL TRIPLE, ADDING EVEN MORE TO THE SUBSTANTIAL *KITTY!*
GRRRR...
OH. SORRY.
OH, I'VE ALWAYS KNOWN I WAS TO BE A GREAT MAN, SMITHERS. I GUESS I'M SIMPLY A *LATE BLOOMER*. THIRTY YEARS OF SERVICE TO THE KWIK-E-MART HAS YIELDED ME BUT ONE THING: *KNOWLEDGE*. KNOWLEDGE AS TO HOW THESE SEMI-ERECT WALKING BUMPKINS THINK. I KNOW THEIR WEAKNESSES, THEIR OBSESSIONS, THEIR HABITS...
IF I CONTINUE TO FOLLOW MY PLAN, WITHIN TWO YEARS EVERY ***PAULY PRUNEJUICE*** AND ***JUDY Q. CROCKPOT*** IN THIS MISERABLE LITTLE BURG WILL QUAKE BEFORE THE ***UNQUESTIONED OMNIPOTENCE*** OF ***C. MONTGOMERY BURNS!***
SPRINGFIELD TIMES
PROJECT RAINBOW: A Plan to Economically Conquer Springfield by C. MONTGOMERY BURNS
ON BECOMING A DESPOT BY ADMIRAL DELPHO KRULL
AUTOMATIC AUTOCRAT 21 Days To Oppressive Power! By Anthony Robbins
ME A MOGUL? HELL, YES! BY KEVIN DEBBS
SMITHERS! GET OFF MY LEG! ***STOP*** THAT!
Lurleen Lumpkin's Roasters TAKE HOME

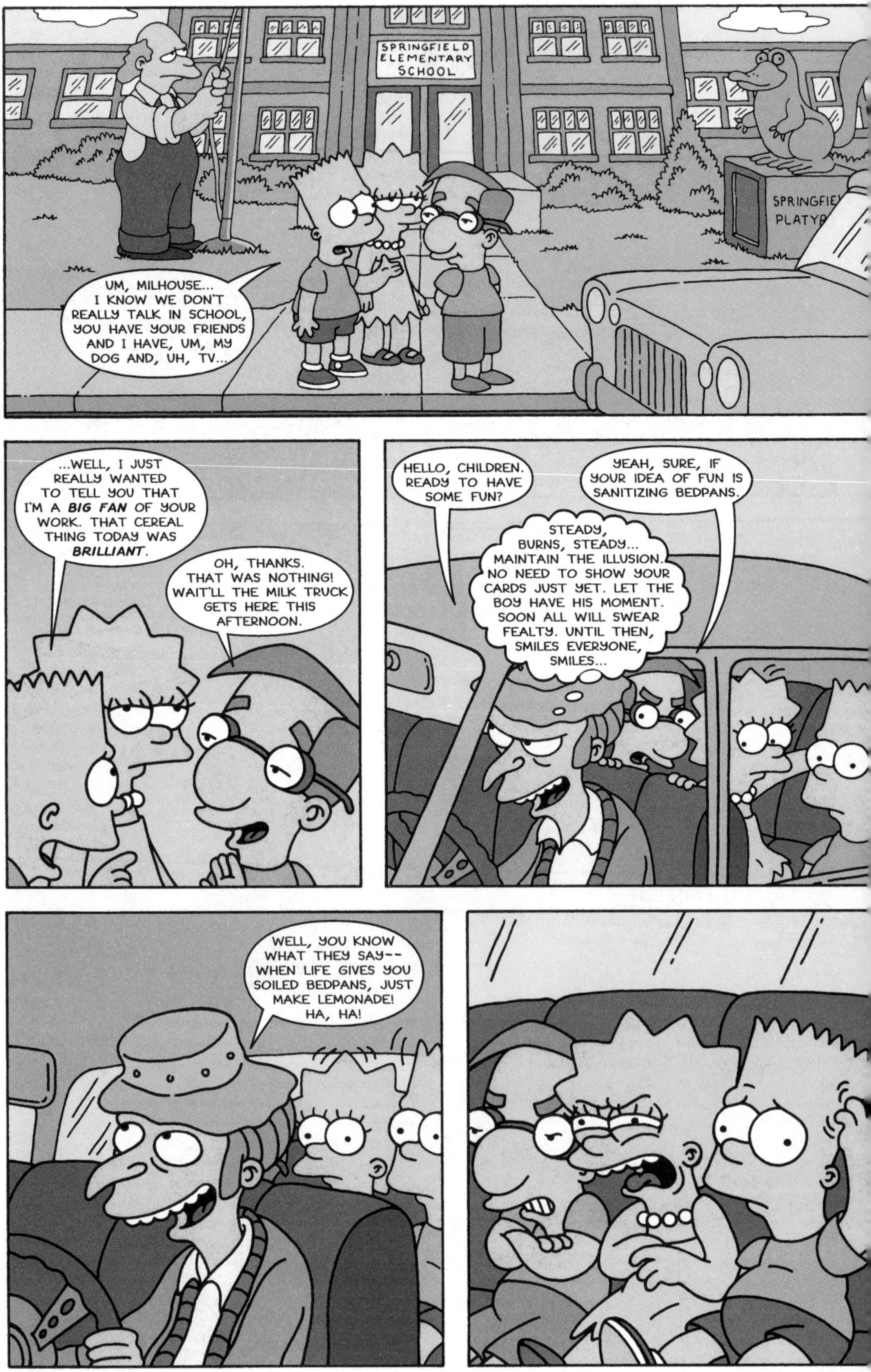
SPRINGFIELD ELEMENTARY SCHOOL
SPRINGFIEL
PLATYP
UM, MILHOUSE... I KNOW WE DON'T REALLY TALK IN SCHOOL, YOU HAVE YOUR FRIENDS AND I HAVE, UM, MY DOG AND, UH, TV...
...WELL, I JUST REALLY WANTED TO TELL YOU THAT I'M A BIG FAN OF YOUR WORK. THAT CEREAL THING TODAY WAS BRILLIANT.
OH, THANKS. THAT WAS NOTHING! WAIT'LL THE MILK TRUCK GETS HERE THIS AFTERNOON.
HELLO, CHILDREN. READY TO HAVE SOME FUN?
YEAH, SURE, IF YOUR IDEA OF FUN IS SANITIZING BEDPANS.
STEADY, BURNS, STEADY... MAINTAIN THE ILLUSION. NO NEED TO SHOW YOUR CARDS JUST YET. LET THE BOY HAVE HIS MOMENT. SOON ALL WILL SWEAR FEALTY. UNTIL THEN, SMILES EVERYONE, SMILES...
WELL, YOU KNOW WHAT THEY SAY-- WHEN LIFE GIVES YOU SOILED BEDPANS, JUST MAKE LEMONADE! HA, HA!

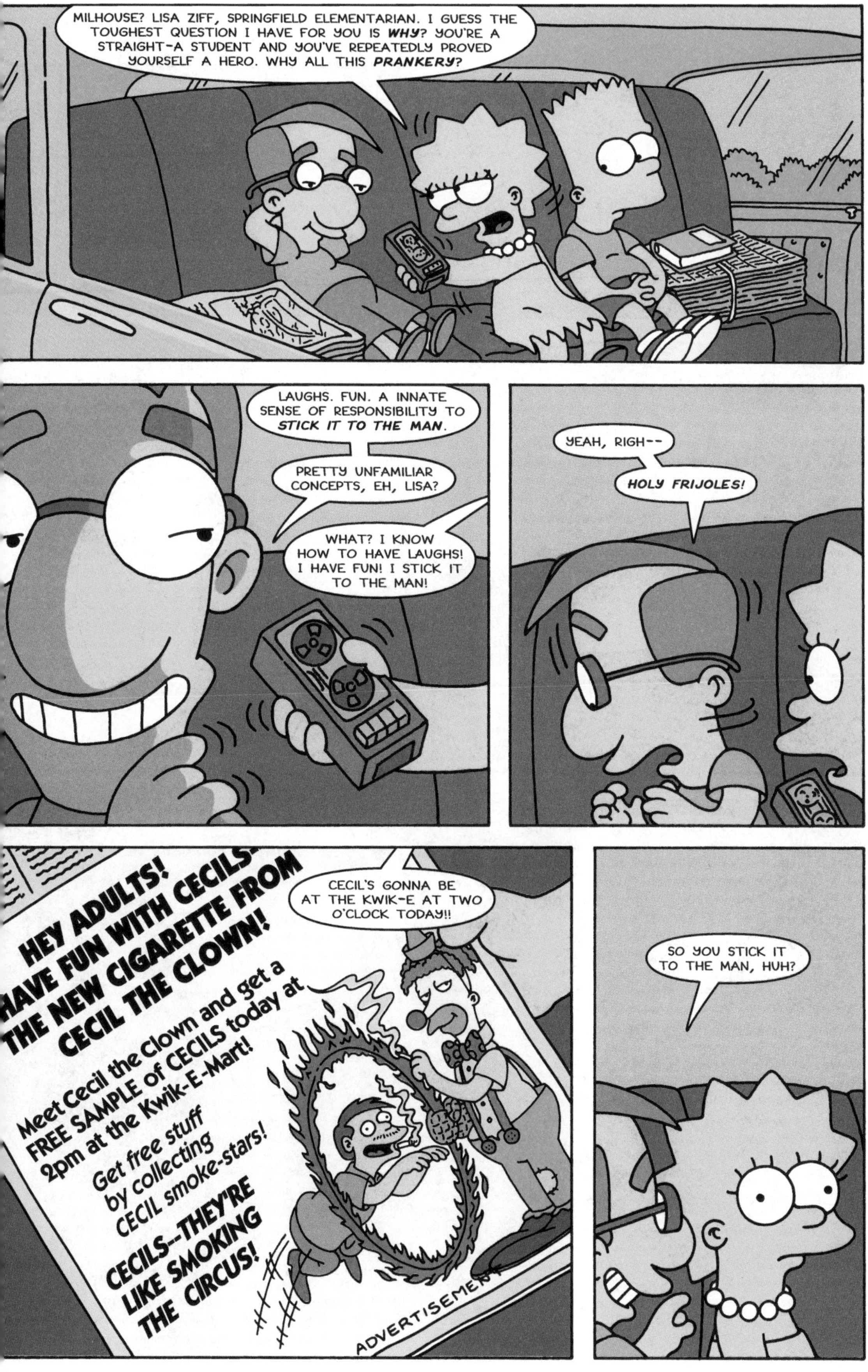
MILHOUSE? LISA ZIFF, SPRINGFIELD ELEMENTARIAN. I GUESS THE TOUGHEST QUESTION I HAVE FOR YOU IS WHY? YOU'RE A STRAIGHT-A STUDENT AND YOU'VE REPEATEDLY PROVED YOURSELF A HERO. WHY ALL THIS PRANKERY?
LAUGHS. FUN. A INNATE SENSE OF RESPONSIBILITY TO STICK IT TO THE MAN.
PRETTY UNFAMILIAR CONCEPTS, EH, LISA?
WHAT? I KNOW HOW TO HAVE LAUGHS! I HAVE FUN! I STICK IT TO THE MAN!
YEAH, RIGH--
HOLY FRIJOLES!
HEY ADULTS! HAVE FUN WITH CECILS- THE NEW CIGARETTE FROM CECIL THE CLOWN!
Meet Cecil the clown and get a FREE SAMPLE of CECILS today at 2pm at the Kwik-E-Mart!
Get free stuff by collecting CECIL smoke-stars!
CECILS--THEY'RE LIKE SMOKING THE CIRCUS!
ADVERTISEMEN
CECIL'S GONNA BE AT THE KWIK-E AT TWO O'CLOCK TODAY!!
SO YOU STICK IT TO THE MAN, HUH?

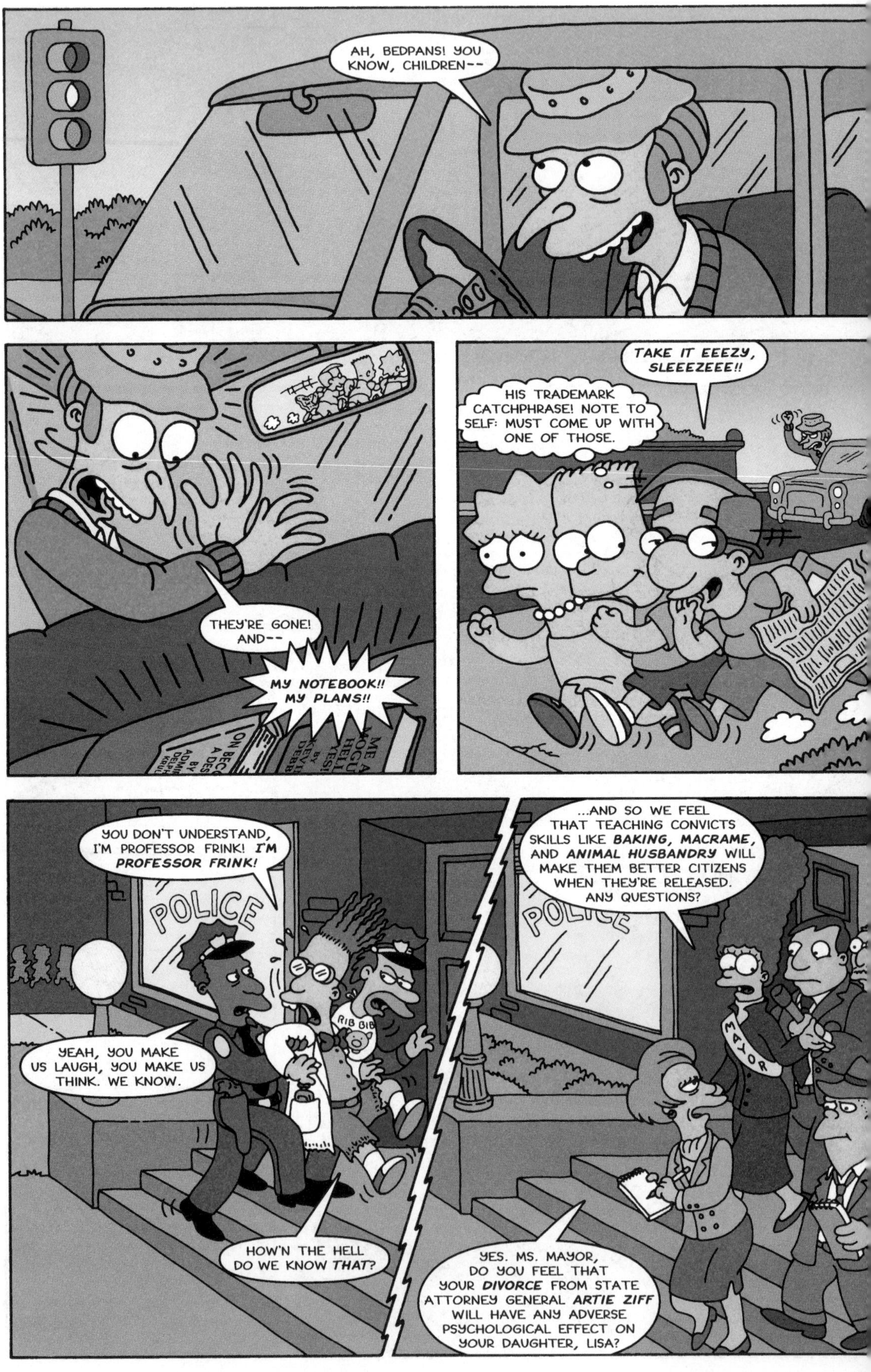
AH, BEDPANS! YOU KNOW, CHILDREN--
THEY'RE GONE! AND--
MY NOTEBOOK!! MY PLANS!!
HIS TRADEMARK CATCHPHRASE! NOTE TO SELF: MUST COME UP WITH ONE OF THOSE.
TAKE IT EEEZY, SLEEEZEEE!!
YOU DON'T UNDERSTAND, I'M PROFESSOR FRINK! I'M PROFESSOR FRINK!
POLICE
YEAH, YOU MAKE US LAUGH, YOU MAKE US THINK. WE KNOW.
RIB BIB
HOW'N THE HELL DO WE KNOW THAT?
...AND SO WE FEEL THAT TEACHING CONVICTS SKILLS LIKE BAKING, MACRAME, AND ANIMAL HUSBANDRY WILL MAKE THEM BETTER CITIZENS WHEN THEY'RE RELEASED. ANY QUESTIONS?
POLICE
MAYOR
YES. MS. MAYOR, DO YOU FEEL THAT YOUR DIVORCE FROM STATE ATTORNEY GENERAL ARTIE ZIFF WILL HAVE ANY ADVERSE PSYCHOLOGICAL EFFECT ON YOUR DAUGHTER, LISA?

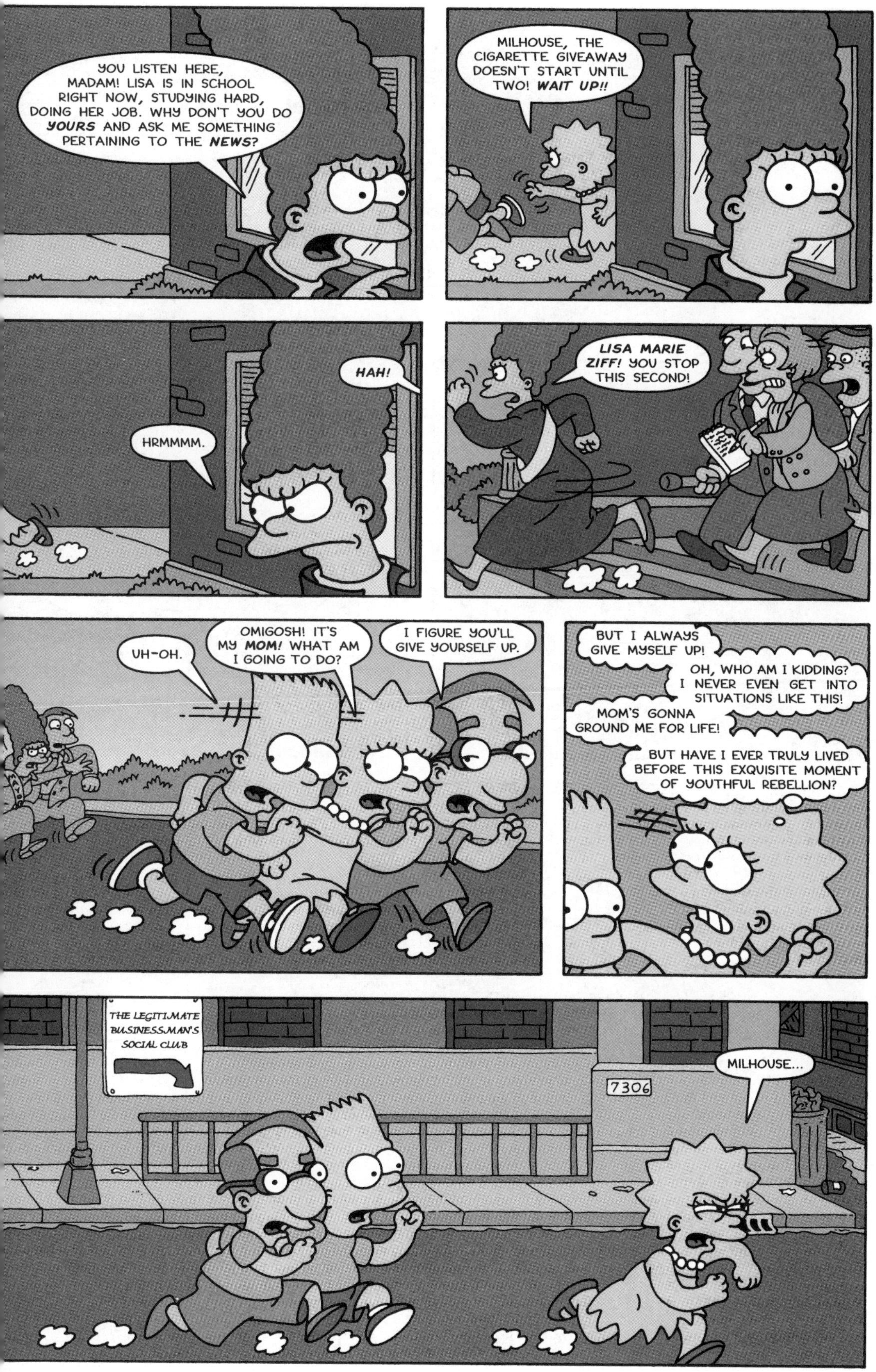
YOU LISTEN HERE, MADAM! LISA IS IN SCHOOL RIGHT NOW, STUDYING HARD, DOING HER JOB. WHY DON'T YOU DO YOURS AND ASK ME SOMETHING PERTAINING TO THE NEWS?
MILHOUSE, THE CIGARETTE GIVEAWAY DOESN'T START UNTIL TWO! WAIT UP!!
HAH!
HRMMMM.
LISA MARIE ZIFF! YOU STOP THIS SECOND!
UH-OH.
OMIGOSH! IT'S MY MOM! WHAT AM I GOING TO DO?
I FIGURE YOU'LL GIVE YOURSELF UP.
BUT I ALWAYS GIVE MYSELF UP!
OH, WHO AM I KIDDING? I NEVER EVEN GET INTO SITUATIONS LIKE THIS!
MOM'S GONNA GROUND ME FOR LIFE!
BUT HAVE I EVER TRULY LIVED BEFORE THIS EXQUISITE MOMENT OF YOUTHFUL REBELLION?
THE LEGITIMATE BUSINESSMAN'S SOCIAL CLUB
7306
MILHOUSE...

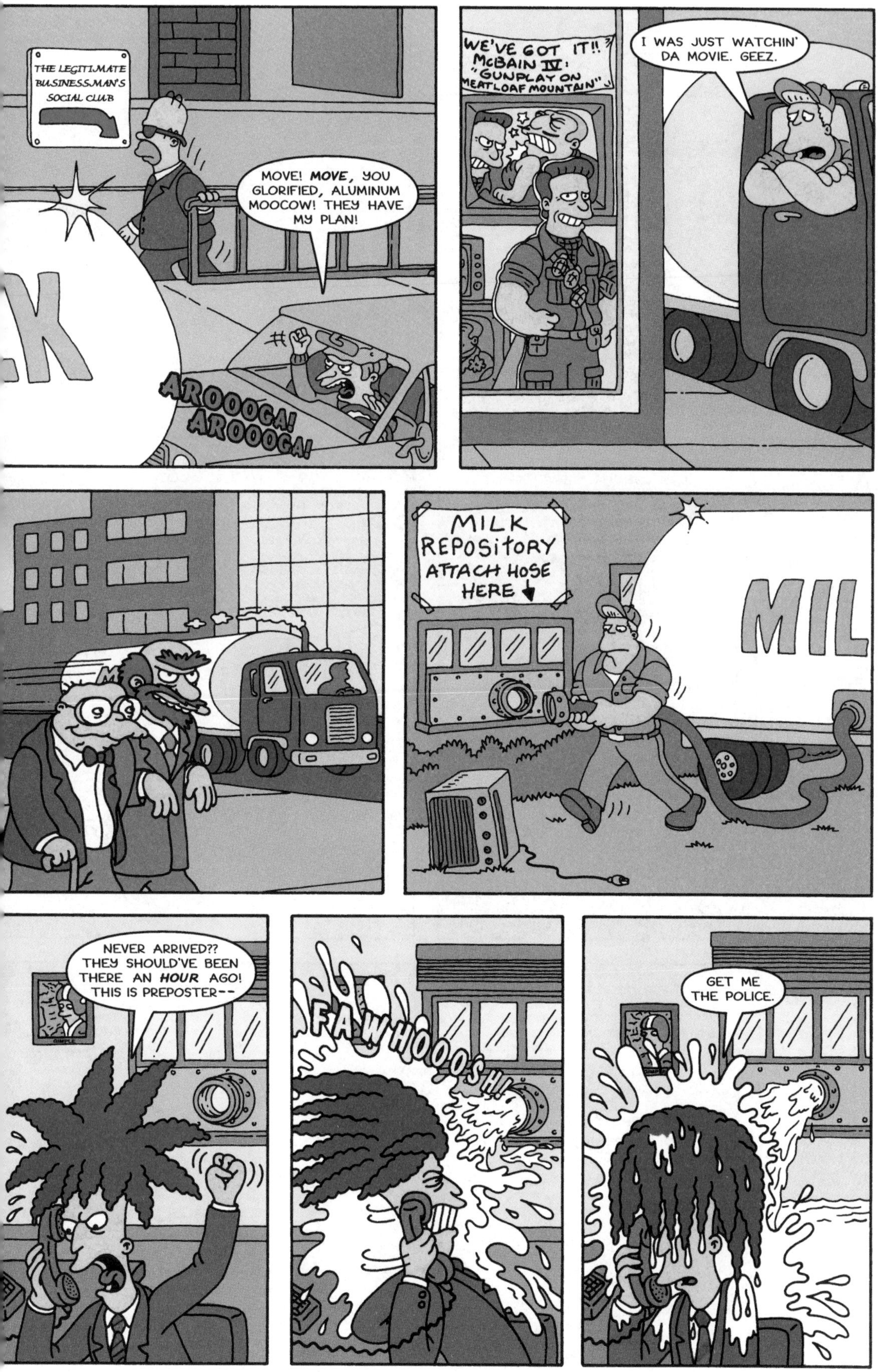
THE LEGITIMATE BUSINESSMAN'S SOCIAL CLUB
MOVE! MOVE, YOU GLORIFIED, ALUMINUM MOOCOW! THEY HAVE MY PLAN!
AROOOGA! AROOOGA!
WE'VE GOT IT!! McBAIN IV: "GUNPLAY ON MEATLOAF MOUNTAIN"
I WAS JUST WATCHIN' DA MOVIE. GEEZ.
MILK REPOSITORY ATTACH HOSE HERE
MIL
NEVER ARRIVED?? THEY SHOULD'VE BEEN THERE AN HOUR AGO! THIS IS PREPOSTER--
FAWHOOOOSH!
GET ME THE POLICE.

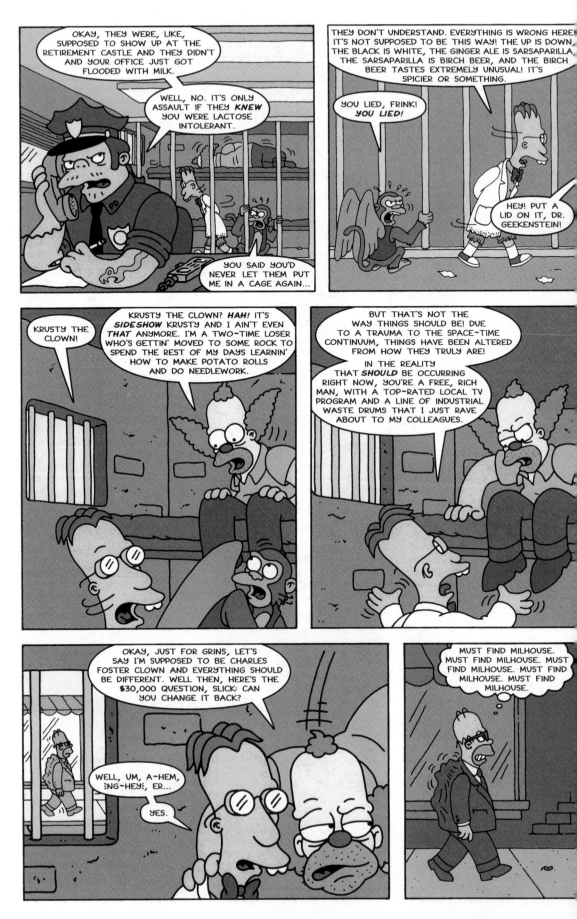

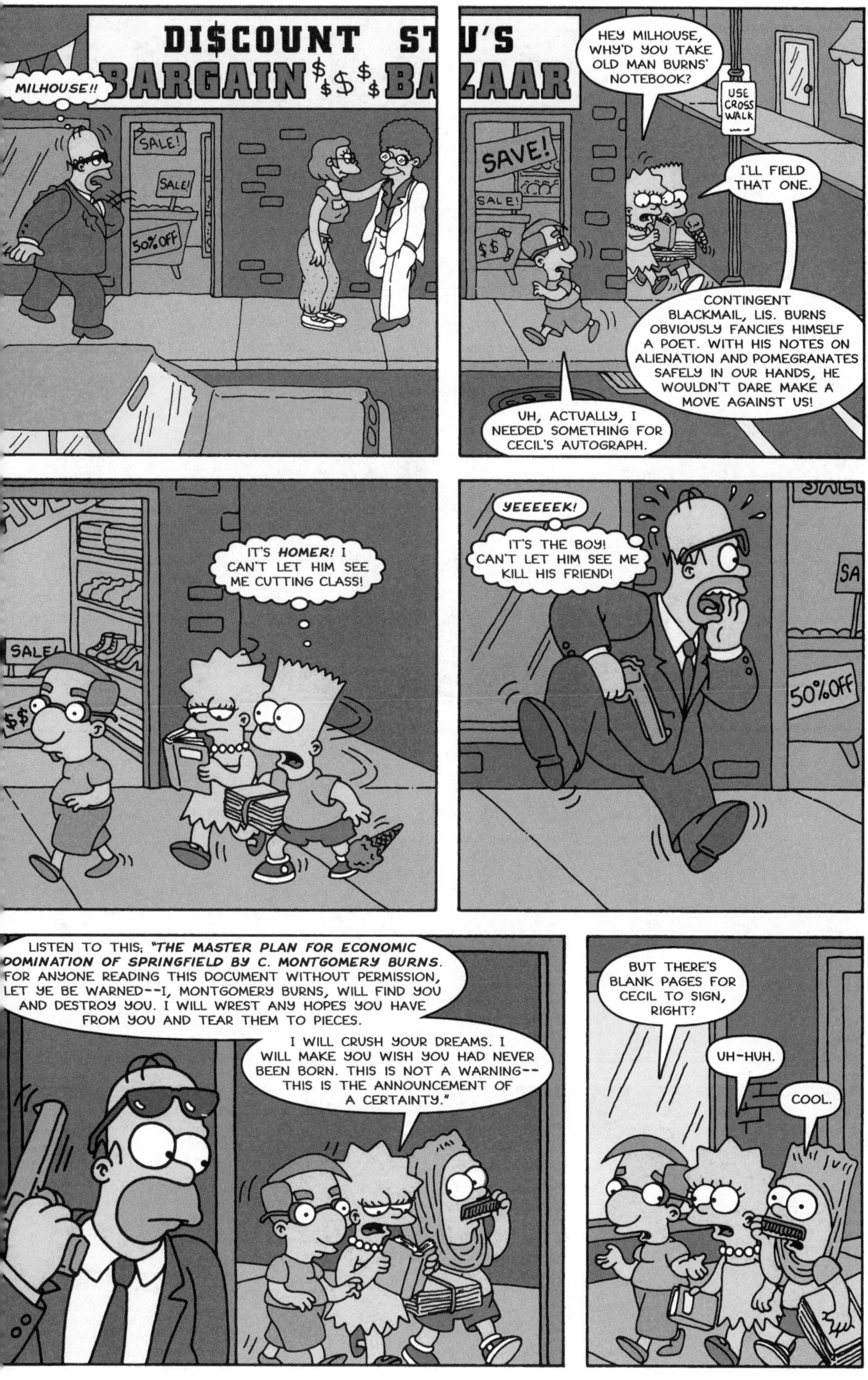
DI$COUNT STU'S BARGAIN $$$$ BAZAAR
MILHOUSE!!
SALE!
SALE!
50% OFF
HEY MILHOUSE, WHY'D YOU TAKE OLD MAN BURNS' NOTEBOOK?
USE CROSS WALK
SAVE!
SALE!
$$
I'LL FIELD THAT ONE.
CONTINGENT BLACKMAIL, LIS. BURNS OBVIOUSLY FANCIES HIMSELF A POET. WITH HIS NOTES ON ALIENATION AND POMEGRANATES SAFELY IN OUR HANDS, HE WOULDN'T DARE MAKE A MOVE AGAINST US!
UH, ACTUALLY, I NEEDED SOMETHING FOR CECIL'S AUTOGRAPH.
SALE!
$$
IT'S HOMER! I CAN'T LET HIM SEE ME CUTTING CLASS!
YEEEEEK!
IT'S THE BOY! CAN'T LET HIM SEE ME KILL HIS FRIEND!
50% OFF
LISTEN TO THIS; "THE MASTER PLAN FOR ECONOMIC DOMINATION OF SPRINGFIELD BY C. MONTGOMERY BURNS. FOR ANYONE READING THIS DOCUMENT WITHOUT PERMISSION, LET YE BE WARNED--I, MONTGOMERY BURNS, WILL FIND YOU AND DESTROY YOU. I WILL WREST ANY HOPES YOU HAVE FROM YOU AND TEAR THEM TO PIECES.
I WILL CRUSH YOUR DREAMS. I WILL MAKE YOU WISH YOU HAD NEVER BEEN BORN. THIS IS NOT A WARNING-- THIS IS THE ANNOUNCEMENT OF A CERTAINTY."
BUT THERE'S BLANK PAGES FOR CECIL TO SIGN, RIGHT?
UH-HUH.
COOL.

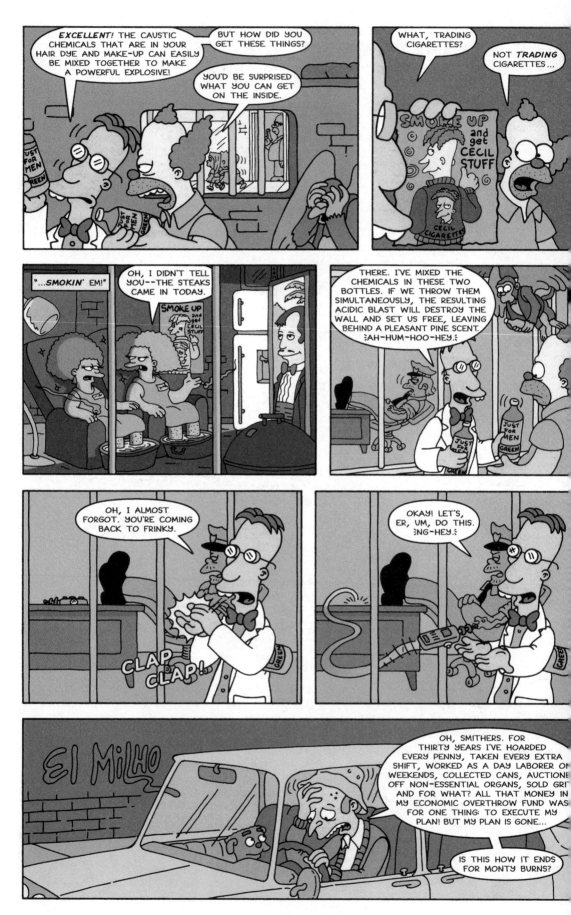

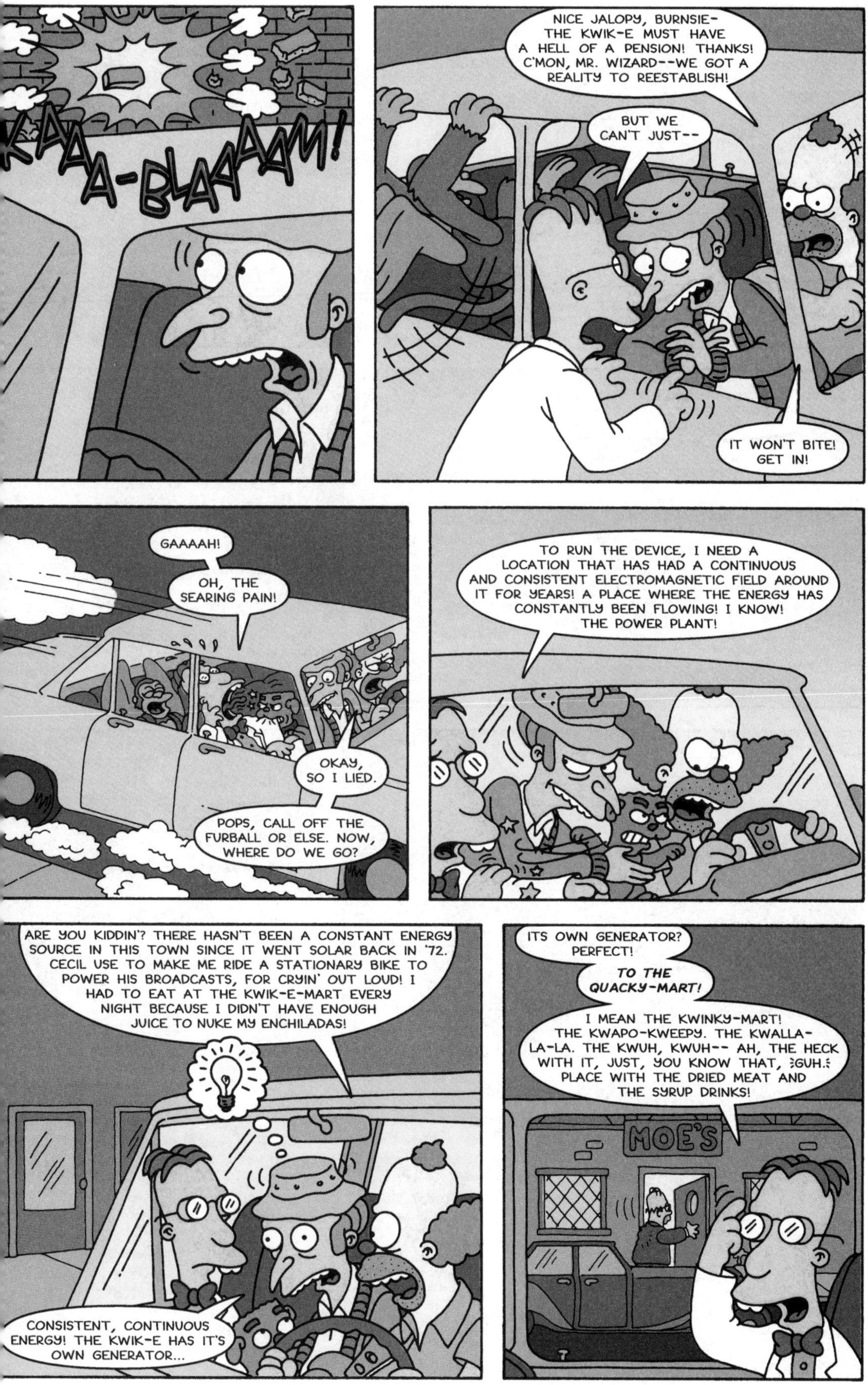
KAAA-BLAAAAM!
NICE JALOPY, BURNSIE- THE KWIK-E MUST HAVE A HELL OF A PENSION! THANKS! C'MON, MR. WIZARD--WE GOT A REALITY TO REESTABLISH!
BUT WE CAN'T JUST--
IT WON'T BITE! GET IN!
GAAAAH!
OH, THE SEARING PAIN!
OKAY, SO I LIED.
POPS, CALL OFF THE FURBALL OR ELSE. NOW, WHERE DO WE GO?
TO RUN THE DEVICE, I NEED A LOCATION THAT HAS HAD A CONTINUOUS AND CONSISTENT ELECTROMAGNETIC FIELD AROUND IT FOR YEARS! A PLACE WHERE THE ENERGY HAS CONSTANTLY BEEN FLOWING! I KNOW! THE POWER PLANT!
ARE YOU KIDDIN'? THERE HASN'T BEEN A CONSTANT ENERGY SOURCE IN THIS TOWN SINCE IT WENT SOLAR BACK IN '72. CECIL USE TO MAKE ME RIDE A STATIONARY BIKE TO POWER HIS BROADCASTS, FOR CRYIN' OUT LOUD! I HAD TO EAT AT THE KWIK-E-MART EVERY NIGHT BECAUSE I DIDN'T HAVE ENOUGH JUICE TO NUKE MY ENCHILADAS!
CONSISTENT, CONTINUOUS ENERGY! THE KWIK-E HAS IT'S OWN GENERATOR...
ITS OWN GENERATOR? PERFECT!
TO THE QUACKY-MART!
I MEAN THE KWINKY-MART! THE KWAPO-KWEEPY. THE KWALLA-LA-LA. THE KWUH, KWUH-- AH, THE HECK WITH IT, JUST, YOU KNOW THAT, GUH. PLACE WITH THE DRIED MEAT AND THE SYRUP DRINKS!
MOE'S

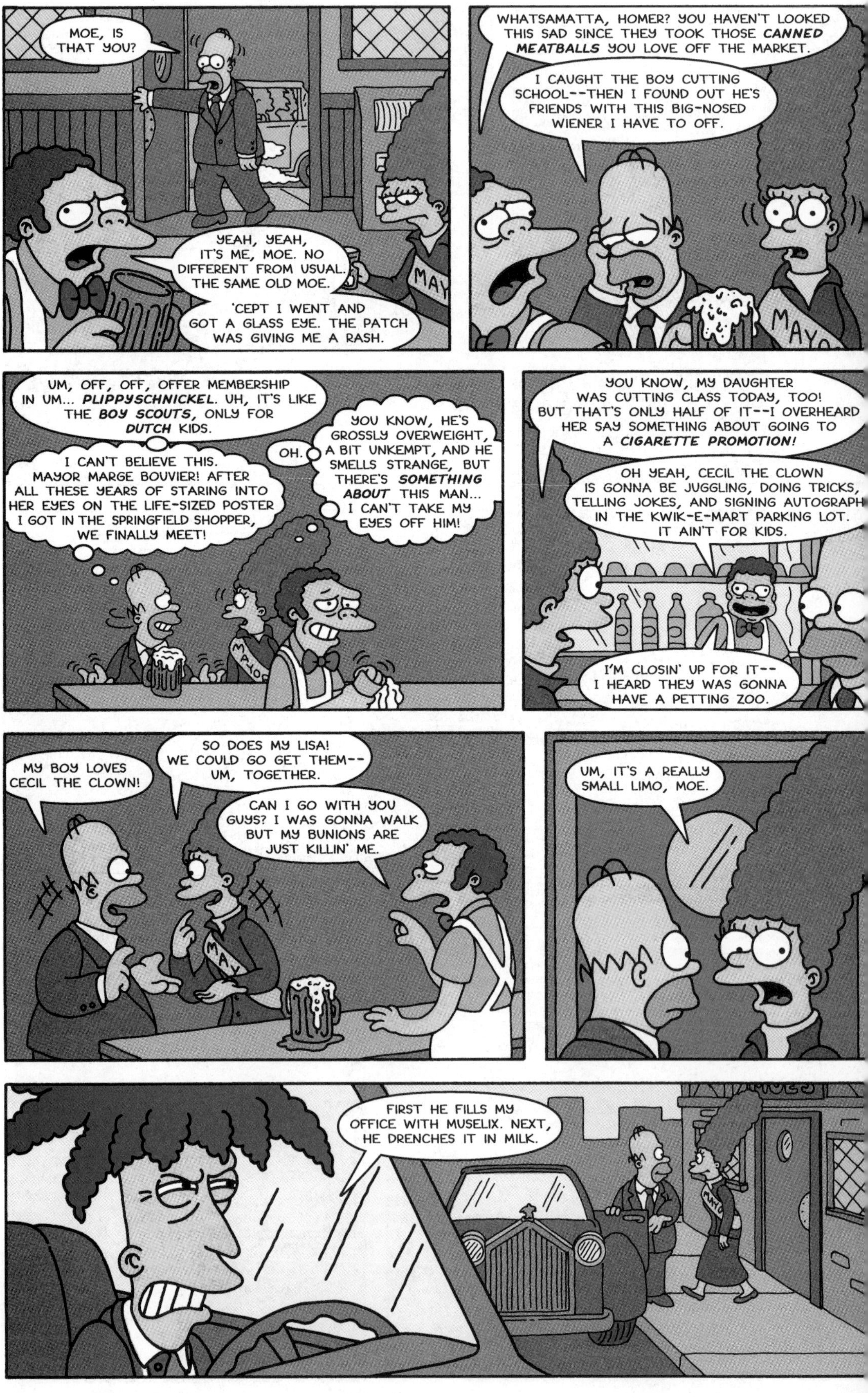
MOE, IS THAT YOU?
YEAH, YEAH, IT'S ME, MOE. NO DIFFERENT FROM USUAL. THE SAME OLD MOE.
'CEPT I WENT AND GOT A GLASS EYE. THE PATCH WAS GIVING ME A RASH.
WHATSAMATTA, HOMER? YOU HAVEN'T LOOKED THIS SAD SINCE THEY TOOK THOSE CANNED MEATBALLS YOU LOVE OFF THE MARKET.
I CAUGHT THE BOY CUTTING SCHOOL--THEN I FOUND OUT HE'S FRIENDS WITH THIS BIG-NOSED WIENER I HAVE TO OFF.
UM, OFF, OFF, OFFER MEMBERSHIP IN UM... PLIPPYSCHNICKEL. UH, IT'S LIKE THE BOY SCOUTS, ONLY FOR DUTCH KIDS.
OH.
I CAN'T BELIEVE THIS. MAYOR MARGE BOUVIER! AFTER ALL THESE YEARS OF STARING INTO HER EYES ON THE LIFE-SIZED POSTER I GOT IN THE SPRINGFIELD SHOPPER, WE FINALLY MEET!
YOU KNOW, HE'S GROSSLY OVERWEIGHT, A BIT UNKEMPT, AND HE SMELLS STRANGE, BUT THERE'S SOMETHING ABOUT THIS MAN... I CAN'T TAKE MY EYES OFF HIM!
YOU KNOW, MY DAUGHTER WAS CUTTING CLASS TODAY, TOO! BUT THAT'S ONLY HALF OF IT--I OVERHEARD HER SAY SOMETHING ABOUT GOING TO A CIGARETTE PROMOTION!
OH YEAH, CECIL THE CLOWN IS GONNA BE JUGGLING, DOING TRICKS, TELLING JOKES, AND SIGNING AUTOGRAPH IN THE KWIK-E-MART PARKING LOT. IT AIN'T FOR KIDS.
I'M CLOSIN' UP FOR IT-- I HEARD THEY WAS GONNA HAVE A PETTING ZOO.
MY BOY LOVES CECIL THE CLOWN!
SO DOES MY LISA! WE COULD GO GET THEM-- UM, TOGETHER.
CAN I GO WITH YOU GUYS? I WAS GONNA WALK BUT MY BUNIONS ARE JUST KILLIN' ME.
UM, IT'S A REALLY SMALL LIMO, MOE.
FIRST HE FILLS MY OFFICE WITH MUSELIX. NEXT, HE DRENCHES IT IN MILK.

FROM THE JOURNAL OF PROFESSOR JOHN FRINK, ENTRY #6270: OOOKAY, LET ME AMEND THAT LAST ENTRY. YES, THE WORLD HAS DANGER APLENTY. BUT THAT YAHTZEE THEOREM WAS PERHAPS A BIT... PREMATURE.

FOR WHATEVER CHAOS SEEMS TO REIGN OVER OUR WORLD, THERE ALSO SEEMS TO BE AN INTRINSIC PATTERN--MUCH LIKE A WAFFLE OR THE WALLPAPER AT THE KRUSTYBURGER--THAT ALL REALITY IS DRAWN TO.

AS A STEPHEN HAWKING PUNCH DOLL WILL ALWAYS RIGHT ITSELF, SO WILL THE WORLD ALWAYS PULL ITSELF TOWARDS THIS PATTERN.

THOUGH THE COSMOS MAY BE SUDDENLY ALTERED AND THROWN ASKEW BY THE OCCASIONAL SUPRA-AMPLIFIED MAGNETIC PULSE-MICROWAVE TINFOIL ACCIDENT, IT TAKES MORE THAN THAT TO COMPLETELY SET ALL CREATION OFF THE COURSE IT IS DETERMINED TO FOLLOW.

TO CONCLUDE, SCIENCE IS A POWERFUL FORCE IN THIS UNIVERSE. BUT WILL THE WORLD ALLOW SCIENCE TO COMPLETELY SCREW IT UP WITH THE MESSING AND THE REORGANIZING AND THE LETTING THINGS HAPPEN THAT SIMPLY CANNOT OCCUR? IN A WORD, NO. SCIENCE MAY DO A LITTLE PUSHING, BUT, MY, OH MY, HOW THE WORLD PUSHES BACK.

THE END

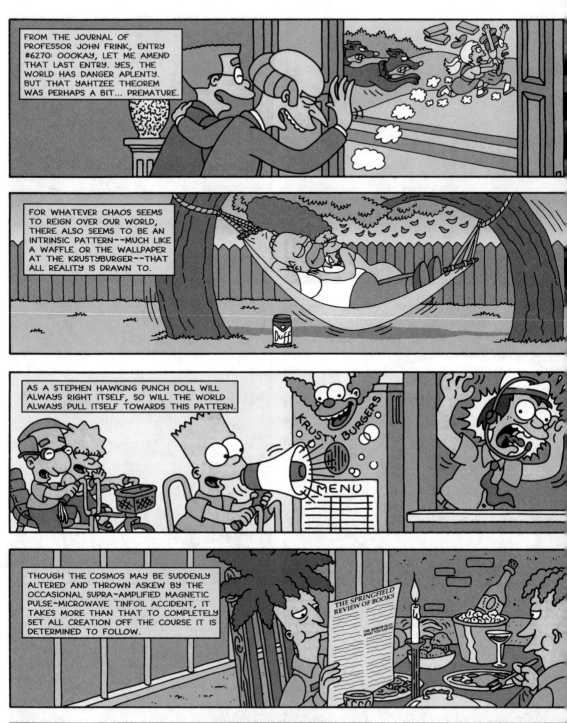

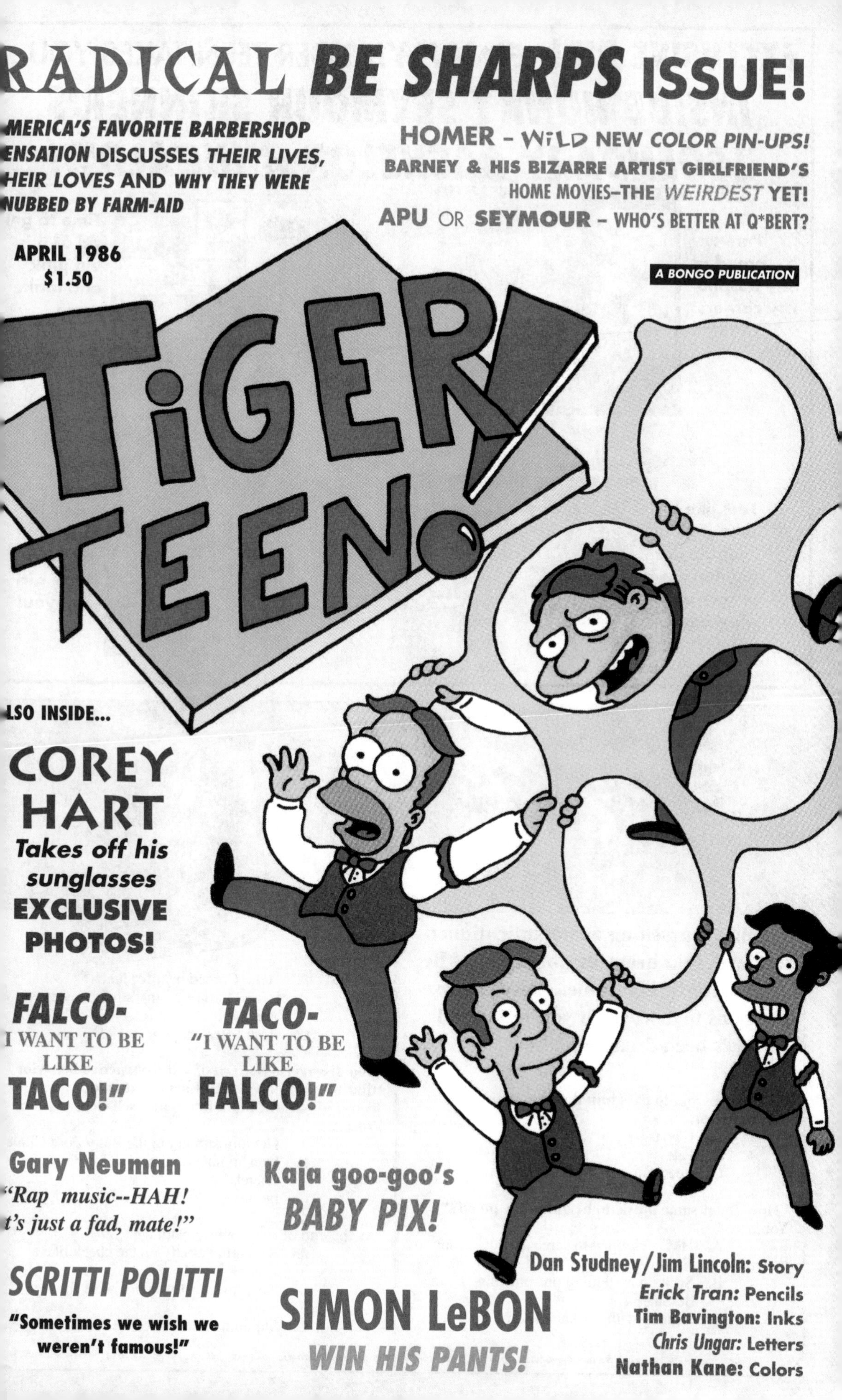

RADICAL BE SHARPS ISSUE!
MERICA'S FAVORITE BARBERSHOP ENSATION DISCUSSES THEIR LIVES, HEIR LOVES AND WHY THEY WERE NUBBED BY FARM-AID
HOMER - WILD NEW COLOR PIN-UPS!
BARNEY & HIS BIZARRE ARTIST GIRLFRIEND'S HOME MOVIES–THE WEIRDEST YET!
APU OR SEYMOUR - WHO'S BETTER AT Q*BERT?
APRIL 1986
$1.50
A BONGO PUBLICATION
TIGER TEEN!
LSO INSIDE...
COREY HART
Takes off his sunglasses
EXCLUSIVE PHOTOS!
FALCO-
I WANT TO BE LIKE TACO!"
TACO-
"I WANT TO BE LIKE FALCO!"
Gary Neuman
'Rap music--HAH! t's just a fad, mate!"
Kaja goo-goo's
BABY PIX!
SCRITTI POLITTI
"Sometimes we wish we weren't famous!"
SIMON LeBON
WIN HIS PANTS!
Dan Studney/Jim Lincoln: Story
Erick Tran: Pencils
Tim Bavington: Inks
Chris Ungar: Letters
Nathan Kane: Colors

EXCLUSIVE PIX! FINALLY! TIGER TEEN TAKES YOU...
INSIDE HUNKY SEYMOUR SKINNER'S LEGENDARY BACHELOR BUNGALOW!

I'm very proud of my hospital corners!

Time to get rid of this old junk and make some room!

Feel like a school girl again in Seymour's private playroom!

This empty chair is just waiting for a girl like you!

Barney's COMPATIBILITY QUIZ!

Imagine yourself on a romantic dinner date with that heart-throbbingest of Be Sharps, Barney Gumble. Answer these questions to discover if you're the girl Barney's been dreaming about!

Barney asks you to pass him the hors d'oeuvres. You reach for...
- A. Caviar
- B. Pate
- C. Beer nuts

"How about some music to heighten the mood?" You...
- A. Hire a violinist to serenade you during dessert
- B. Suck up by putting on something by the Be-Sharps
- C. Sign up with the karaoke guy

"Braaap!!"
- A. "Oh. Corned beef for lunch?"
- B. "Good lord of all that's holy, my eyes are burning!"
- C. "Can I freshen your drink?"

You discover a pattern of self-destructive behavior that will ultimately lead Barney into a downward spiral of shame, humiliation and self-degradation. You...
- A. Get him straight to the Betty Ford Clinic
- B. Plan an intervention with his closest friends
- C. Ignore it

At the end of the evening, you...
- A. Kiss him sweetly on the cheek like a sister
- B. Hold him tightly as if it were the last time
- C. Slip him twenty bucks

If you answered 'C' to any or all of these questions, you are compatible with Barney. If 'A' or 'B' - you are compatible with the rest of the world.

OMER SIMPSON

answers 40 intimate questions

What are your hobbies?
I enjoy poker with the boys, television, drinking beer, and safety dancing.

Why do you prefer not to talk about your marriage?
Marriage? I'm not married! Who told you I was married? That's ridiculous. I'm an eligible young bachelor with a swingin' single lifestyle. Just ask my wife, Marge. D'oh!!

Is it true that you don't care if you're called a square?
Hey, if loving barbershop is square, I don't want to be round...man.

You were a nuclear safety inspector before you became a professional singer. How are the jobs different?
Well, it's not too different. At the plant, I used to sneak into the broom closet to wear funny hats and sing to myself. I guess the only difference is that now I'm out of the closet. You can quote me on that!

What's the history of barbershop singing?
Who do I look like, the freakin' Shell answer man? No, seriously...because people are always saying, "You look like that Shell guy!" What was the question again?

Word on the street is that you're a big donut fan. If you were a donut, what kind would you be?
Hmm... Well for one thing, I'd have sprinkles. And frosting. I'd be fashionably powdered and I would contain both jelly and cream. I would weigh over two hundred pounds and be chocolate rippled. There would be statues of me at baking schools and I would be served with fourteen gallons of milk! I would come with an extra bucket of sugar! People would compose songs about me! They'd make a tv movie about my life story! People would proclaim me Carby, King of the Donut Men. But I digress. I believe your original question had to do with some mythical donut street...?

Do you think the group will ever split up?
As long as they're putting music on vinyl, the Be Sharps will be there to record it.

Who are your favorite singers?
Ray Stevens has had a profound effect on me. The Doodletown Pipers are easily the world's greatest band. Of course, Grand Funk Railroad's music has been the soundtrack for my life and they opened up my mind to the possibility of time travel and inspired my lifelong dream--to build the world's biggest tom-tom.

Who is your favorite actor?
Oh, that guy...you know, the guy with the show. The one with the hair and the leg thingy.

What is your favorite food?
Pork chops, donuts, honey-roasted peanuts, my patented space-age moon waffles, ice cream cakes, Krusty burgers, Krusty burgers with cheese, Double Krusty burgers, frozen Salisbury steak dinners, corn dogs, Duff beer, beer nuts, pretzels, popcorn, cotton candy, vegimite sandwiches, anything with caramel coating, that stuff from France in the funny package, syrup, pudding roll-ups, chocolate, chocolate bars, chocolate kisses, chocolate milk, crumbled-up chocolatey things. Mmm...chocolate. This interview is over!

APU DE BEAUMARCHAIS

--LICK HIS TEARS AWAY

IN THE SECRET HEART of Apu de Beaumarchais, there is a corner with the word SORROW written on it. If you love Apu and would like to truly help lick his tears away (metaphorically, of course--tears have been proven to contain strains of certain viruses and Tiger Teen assumes no liability in the actual licking thereof), listen as he tells you about the things a girl can do to make him happy.

For a woman to give the awful, dark sadness in my soul the "rush of the bum", she will have to be a woman who concerns herself with the small, intimate details of life. A smile. A touch. The ever-so important freshness dating on dairy products.

Much of my tormented misery comes from a lack of inner harmony and balance, along with an unnatural fear of large denominations of currency. If you were my friend and cared enough, when out shopping with me, you would always have exact change and use no bills larger than a twenty please.

But the best way to shine a bright light into the ever-expanding blackness that eats away at my very being is a simple thing--always be open. Anyone who wishes to stop the flow of my salty tears will be conveniently available to me twenty-four hours a day. Including weekends and holidays. Thank you and come again.

EDNA KRABAPPEL grades *THE BE SHARPS*

Only one diehard dame in all of Springfield can lay claim to being a Be Sharps groupie from their earliest days back at Moe's Cavern--*Edna Krabappel.*

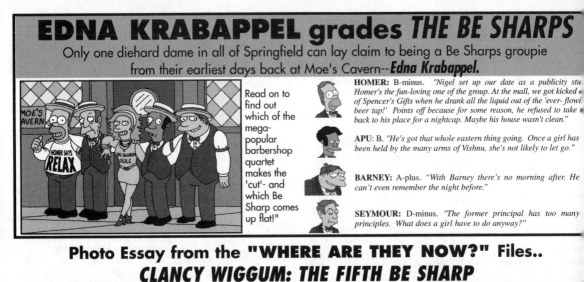

Read on to find out which of the mega-popular barbershop quartet makes the 'cut'- and which Be Sharp comes up flat!"

HOMER: B-minus. *"Nigel set up our date as a publicity stu Homer's the fun-loving one of the group. At the mall, we got kicked of Spencer's Gifts when he drank all the liquid out of the 'ever-flowi beer tap!' Points off because for some reason, he refused to take back to his place for a nightcap. Maybe his house wasn't clean."*

APU: B. *"He's got that whole eastern thing going. Once a girl has been held by the many arms of Vishnu, she's not likely to let go."*

BARNEY: A-plus. *"With Barney there's no morning after. He can't even remember the night before."*

SEYMOUR: D-minus. *"The former principal has too many principles. What does a girl have to do anyway?"*

Photo Essay from the "WHERE ARE THEY NOW?" Files..
CLANCY WIGGUM: THE FIFTH BE SHARP

After being booted out of the Be Sharps, Wiggum started his own group: The Barber-Cop Quartet. The video from their single, 'Revolution No. 9-1-1' never achieved heavy rotation on the MTV chart.

After the inevitable break-up, Clancy fell in with the wrong crowd, all desperately seeking to relive their former celebrity.

We spoke to Clancy by phone. He ha this to say: "No, I'm not bitter. I alway know deep in my heart that no matte what terrible things I've done, there always a place for me right here in the Springfield Police Department."

Even as we go to press, the *Be Sharps* are hard at work on their first-ever feature-length movie--

Featuring 5 new songs that are bound to be classic 80's hits!
- Strawberry Lip Gloss Forever
- Faxman
- Being for the Benefit of Mr. T.
- Give Beta a Chance
- Mean Mr. Myagi
- The Ballad of Crockett & Tubbs
- Your Mother Should Just Say No
- Pac-Man Pam
- Everybody's Got Something to Hide (Except Me and Moncchichi)

Hitting multiplexes just in time for Christmas!

COMICS BONGO GROUP
#34
US $2.25
CAN $2.95
SIMPSONS
COMICS
©1997 BONGO ENTERTAINMENT, INC. THE SIMPSONS ©&TM TWENTIETH CENTURY FOX FILM CORPORATION. ALL RIGHTS RESERVED.
MATT GROENING

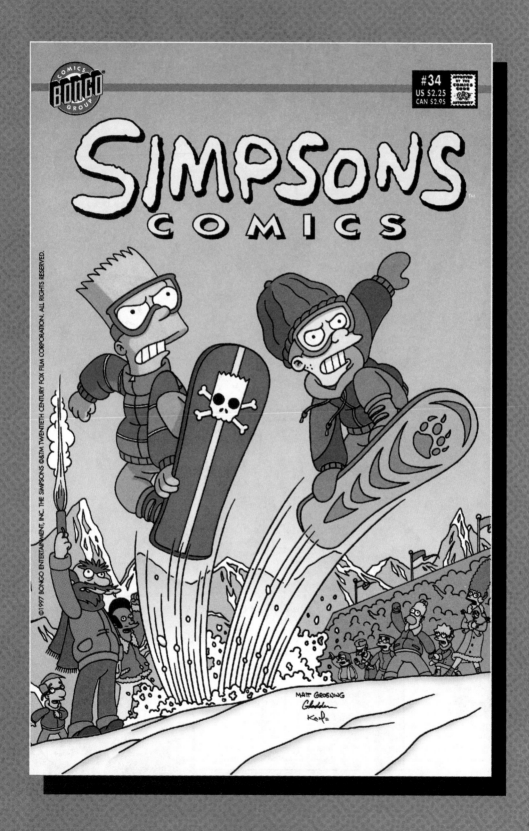

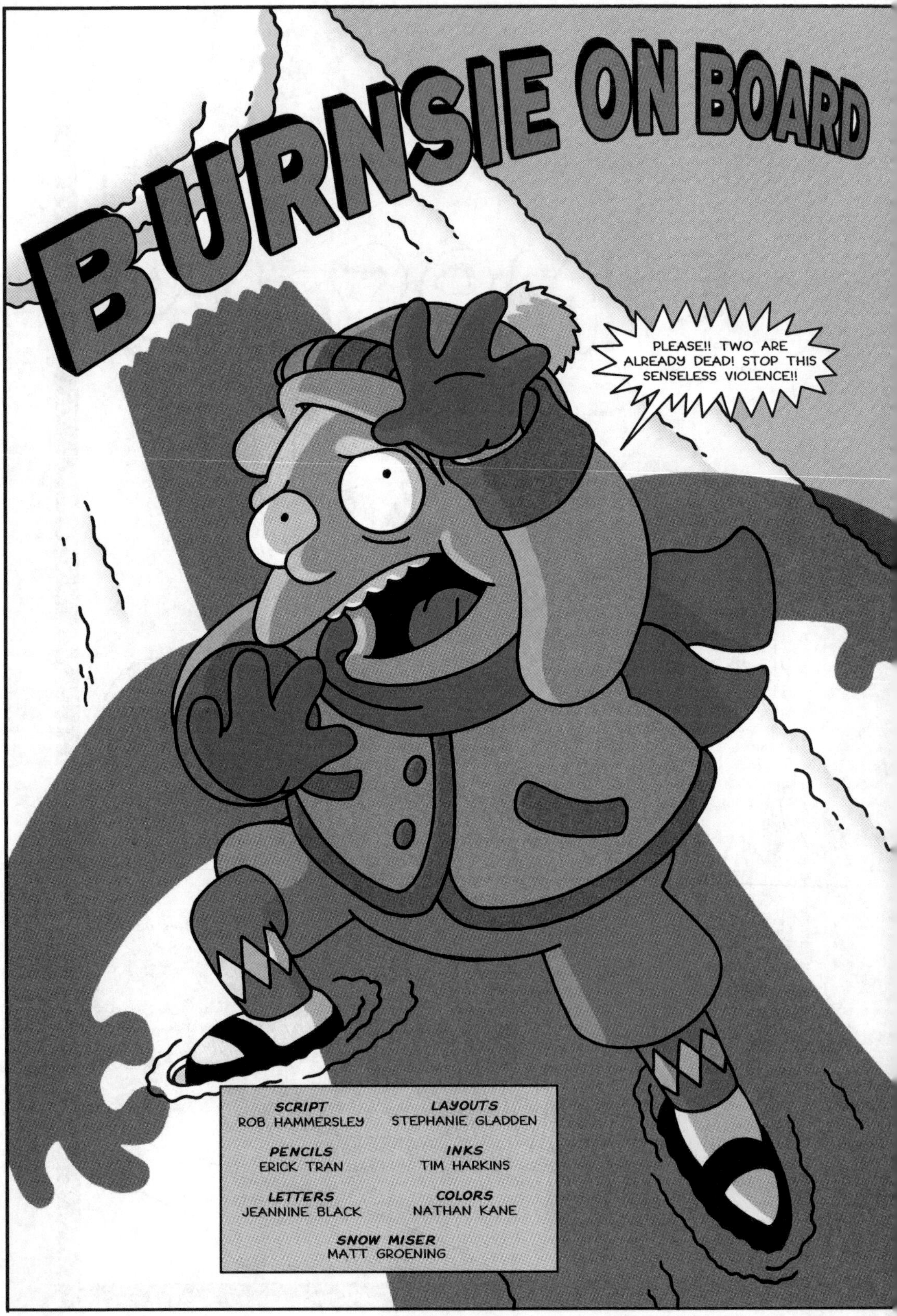

BURNSIE ON BOARD
PLEASE!! TWO ARE ALREADY DEAD! STOP THIS SENSELESS VIOLENCE!!
SCRIPT
ROB HAMMERSLEY
LAYOUTS
STEPHANIE GLADDEN
PENCILS
ERICK TRAN
INKS
TIM HARKINS
LETTERS
JEANNINE BLACK
COLORS
NATHAN KANE
SNOW MISER
MATT GROENING

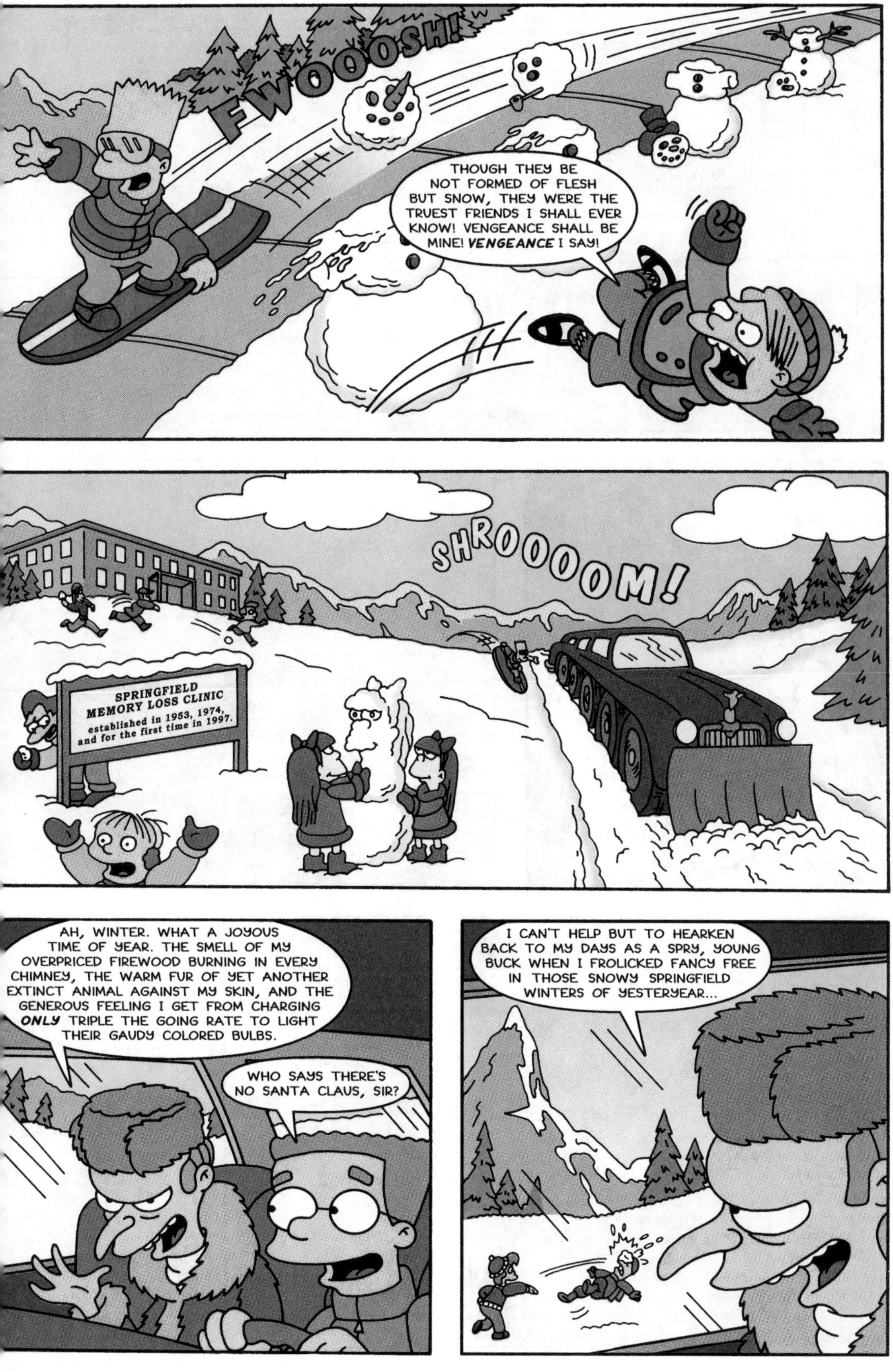
FWOOOSH!
THOUGH THEY BE NOT FORMED OF FLESH BUT SNOW, THEY WERE THE TRUEST FRIENDS I SHALL EVER KNOW! VENGEANCE SHALL BE MINE! VENGEANCE I SAY!
SHROOOOOM!
SPRINGFIELD MEMORY LOSS CLINIC established in 1953, 1974, and for the first time in 1997.
AH, WINTER. WHAT A JOYOUS TIME OF YEAR. THE SMELL OF MY OVERPRICED FIREWOOD BURNING IN EVERY CHIMNEY, THE WARM FUR OF YET ANOTHER EXTINCT ANIMAL AGAINST MY SKIN, AND THE GENEROUS FEELING I GET FROM CHARGING ONLY TRIPLE THE GOING RATE TO LIGHT THEIR GAUDY COLORED BULBS.
WHO SAYS THERE'S NO SANTA CLAUS, SIR?
I CAN'T HELP BUT TO HEARKEN BACK TO MY DAYS AS A SPRY, YOUNG BUCK WHEN I FROLICKED FANCY FREE IN THOSE SNOWY SPRINGFIELD WINTERS OF YESTERYEAR...

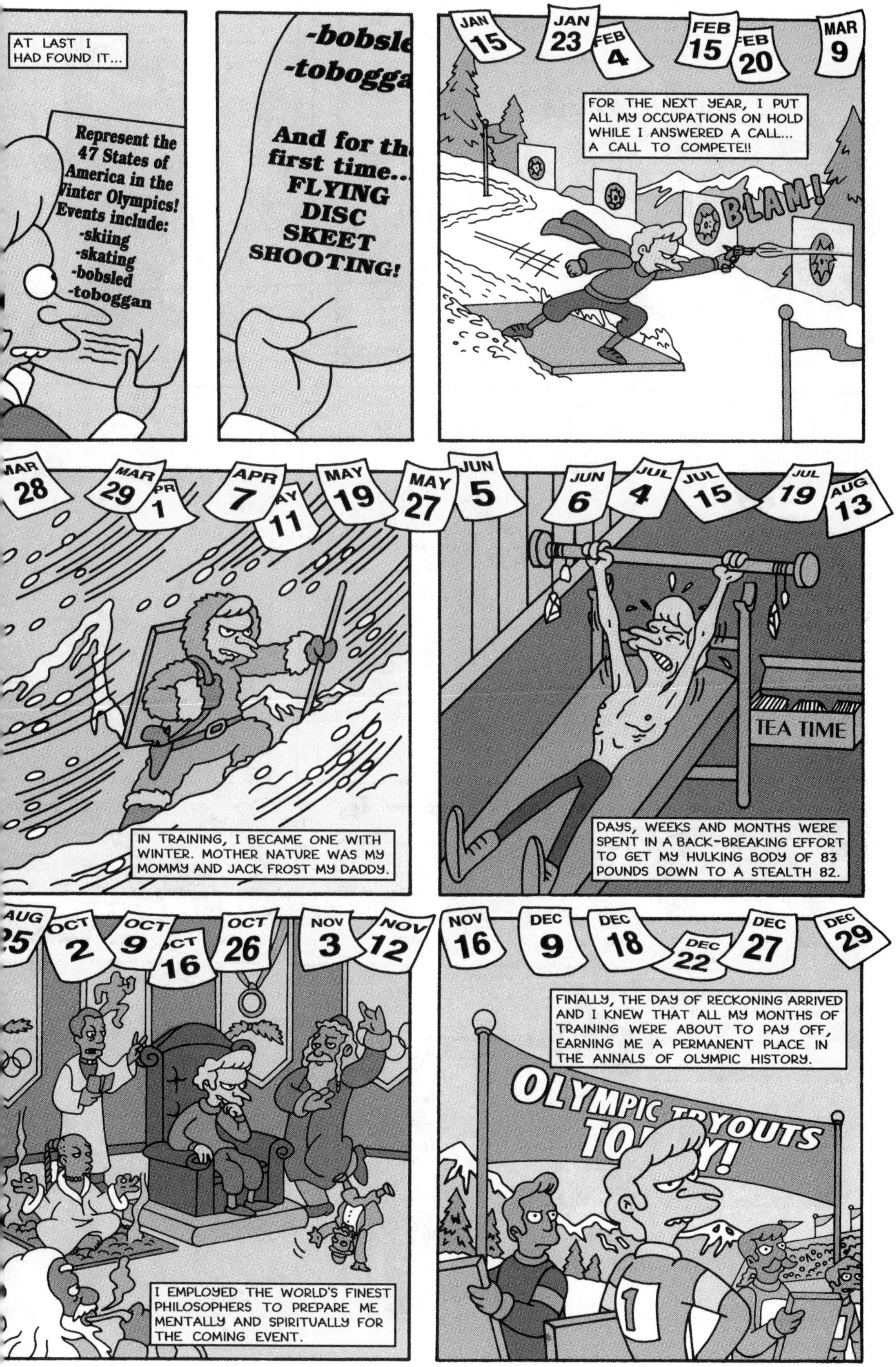
AT LAST I HAD FOUND IT...
Represent the 47 States of America in the Winter Olympics! Events include: -skiing -skating -bobsled -toboggan
-bobsle
-tobogga
And for th first time... FLYING DISC SKEET SHOOTING!
JAN 15
JAN 23
FEB 4
FEB 15
FEB 20
MAR 9
FOR THE NEXT YEAR, I PUT ALL MY OCCUPATIONS ON HOLD WHILE I ANSWERED A CALL... A CALL TO COMPETE!!
BLAM!
MAR 28
MAR 29
APR 1
APR 7
MAY 11
MAY 19
MAY 27
JUN 5
IN TRAINING, I BECAME ONE WITH WINTER. MOTHER NATURE WAS MY MOMMY AND JACK FROST MY DADDY.
JUN 6
JUL 4
JUL 15
JUL 19
AUG 13
TEA TIME
DAYS, WEEKS AND MONTHS WERE SPENT IN A BACK-BREAKING EFFORT TO GET MY HULKING BODY OF 83 POUNDS DOWN TO A STEALTH 82.
AUG 25
OCT 2
OCT 9
OCT 16
OCT 26
NOV 3
NOV 12
I EMPLOYED THE WORLD'S FINEST PHILOSOPHERS TO PREPARE ME MENTALLY AND SPIRITUALLY FOR THE COMING EVENT.
NOV 16
DEC 9
DEC 18
DEC 22
DEC 27
DEC 29
FINALLY, THE DAY OF RECKONING ARRIVED AND I KNEW THAT ALL MY MONTHS OF TRAINING WERE ABOUT TO PAY OFF, EARNING ME A PERMANENT PLACE IN THE ANNALS OF OLYMPIC HISTORY.
OLYMPIC TRYOUTS TO Y!
1

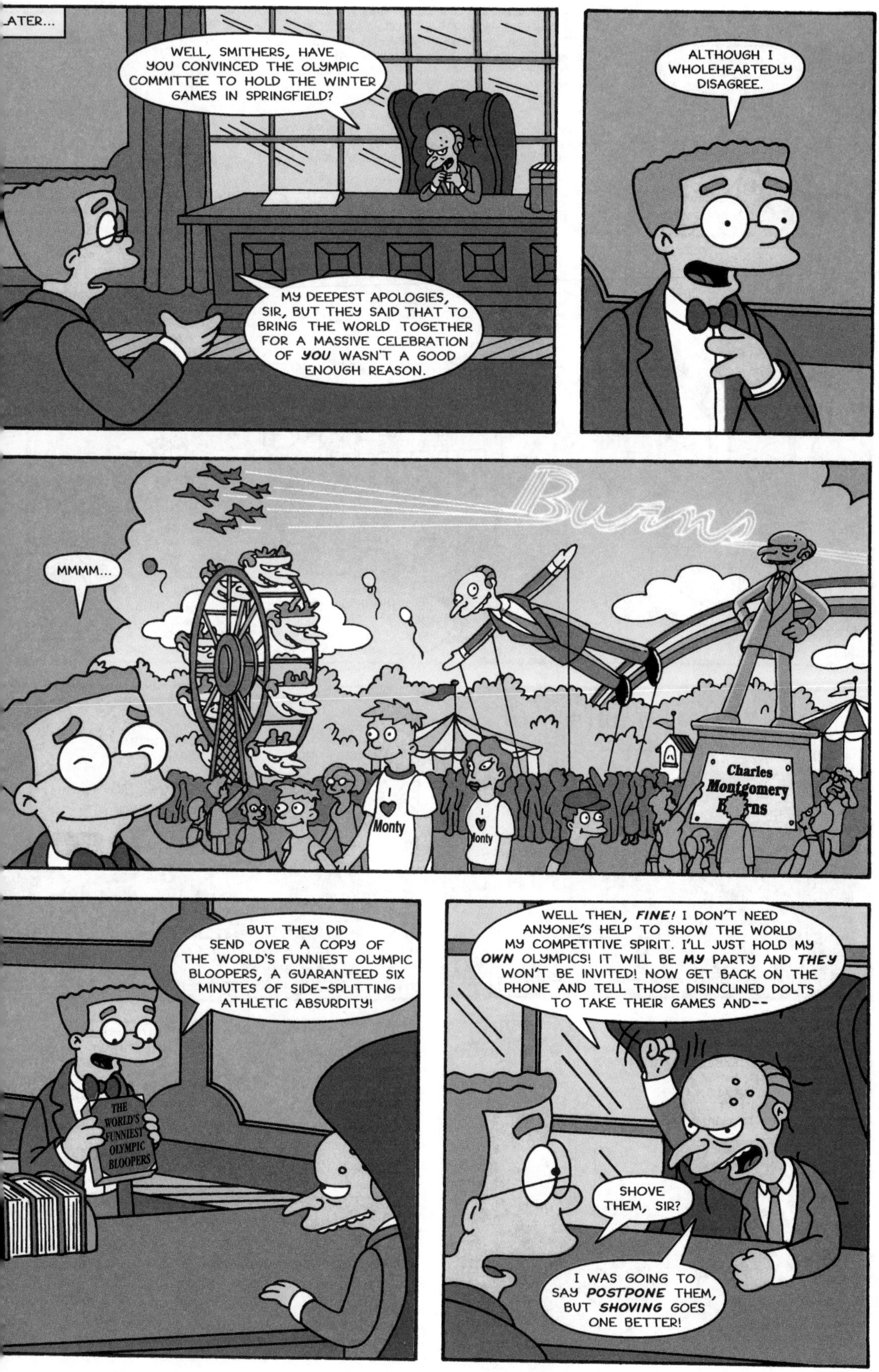
LATER...
WELL, SMITHERS, HAVE YOU CONVINCED THE OLYMPIC COMMITTEE TO HOLD THE WINTER GAMES IN SPRINGFIELD?
MY DEEPEST APOLOGIES, SIR, BUT THEY SAID THAT TO BRING THE WORLD TOGETHER FOR A MASSIVE CELEBRATION OF YOU WASN'T A GOOD ENOUGH REASON.
ALTHOUGH I WHOLEHEARTEDLY DISAGREE.
MMMM...
Burns
Monty
Monty
Charles Montgomery Burns
BUT THEY DID SEND OVER A COPY OF THE WORLD'S FUNNIEST OLYMPIC BLOOPERS, A GUARANTEED SIX MINUTES OF SIDE-SPLITTING ATHLETIC ABSURDITY!
THE WORLD'S FUNNIEST OLYMPIC BLOOPERS
WELL THEN, FINE! I DON'T NEED ANYONE'S HELP TO SHOW THE WORLD MY COMPETITIVE SPIRIT. I'LL JUST HOLD MY OWN OLYMPICS! IT WILL BE MY PARTY AND THEY WON'T BE INVITED! NOW GET BACK ON THE PHONE AND TELL THOSE DISINCLINED DOLTS TO TAKE THEIR GAMES AND--
SHOVE THEM, SIR?
I WAS GOING TO SAY POSTPONE THEM, BUT SHOVING GOES ONE BETTER!

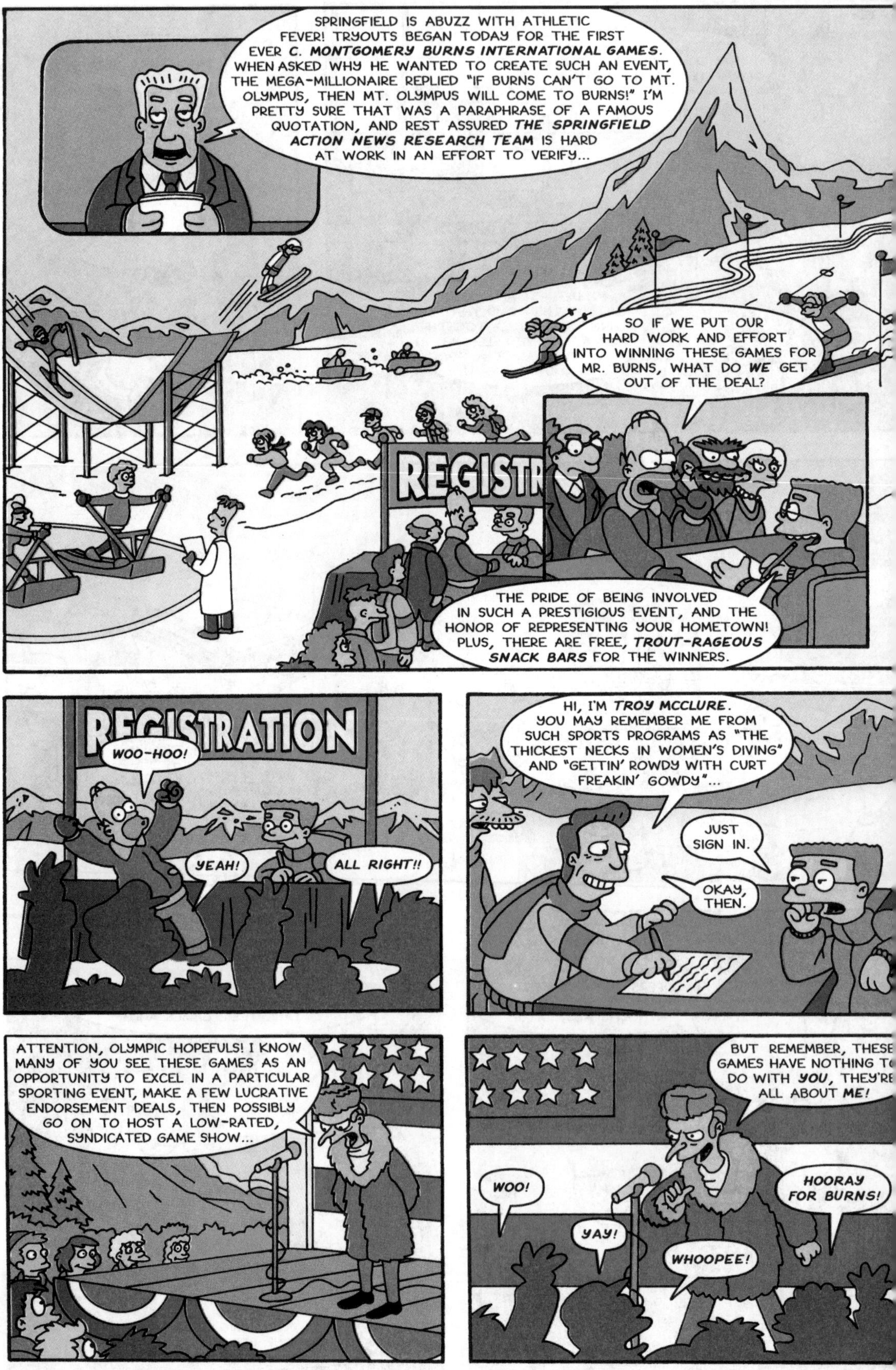
SPRINGFIELD IS ABUZZ WITH ATHLETIC FEVER! TRYOUTS BEGAN TODAY FOR THE FIRST EVER ***C. MONTGOMERY BURNS INTERNATIONAL GAMES***. WHEN ASKED WHY HE WANTED TO CREATE SUCH AN EVENT, THE MEGA-MILLIONAIRE REPLIED "IF BURNS CAN'T GO TO MT. OLYMPUS, THEN MT. OLYMPUS WILL COME TO BURNS!" I'M PRETTY SURE THAT WAS A PARAPHRASE OF A FAMOUS QUOTATION, AND REST ASSURED ***THE SPRINGFIELD ACTION NEWS RESEARCH TEAM*** IS HARD AT WORK IN AN EFFORT TO VERIFY...
SO IF WE PUT OUR HARD WORK AND EFFORT INTO WINNING THESE GAMES FOR MR. BURNS, WHAT DO ***WE*** GET OUT OF THE DEAL?
REGISTR
THE PRIDE OF BEING INVOLVED IN SUCH A PRESTIGIOUS EVENT, AND THE HONOR OF REPRESENTING YOUR HOMETOWN! PLUS, THERE ARE FREE, ***TROUT-RAGEOUS SNACK BARS*** FOR THE WINNERS.
REGISTRATION
WOO-HOO!
YEAH!
ALL RIGHT!!
HI, I'M ***TROY MCCLURE***. YOU MAY REMEMBER ME FROM SUCH SPORTS PROGRAMS AS "THE THICKEST NECKS IN WOMEN'S DIVING" AND "GETTIN' ROWDY WITH CURT FREAKIN' GOWDY"...
JUST SIGN IN.
OKAY, THEN.
ATTENTION, OLYMPIC HOPEFULS! I KNOW MANY OF YOU SEE THESE GAMES AS AN OPPORTUNITY TO EXCEL IN A PARTICULAR SPORTING EVENT, MAKE A FEW LUCRATIVE ENDORSEMENT DEALS, THEN POSSIBLY GO ON TO HOST A LOW-RATED, SYNDICATED GAME SHOW...
BUT REMEMBER, THESE GAMES HAVE NOTHING TO DO WITH ***YOU***, THEY'RE ALL ABOUT ***ME!***
WOO!
YAY!
WHOOPEE!
HOORAY FOR BURNS!

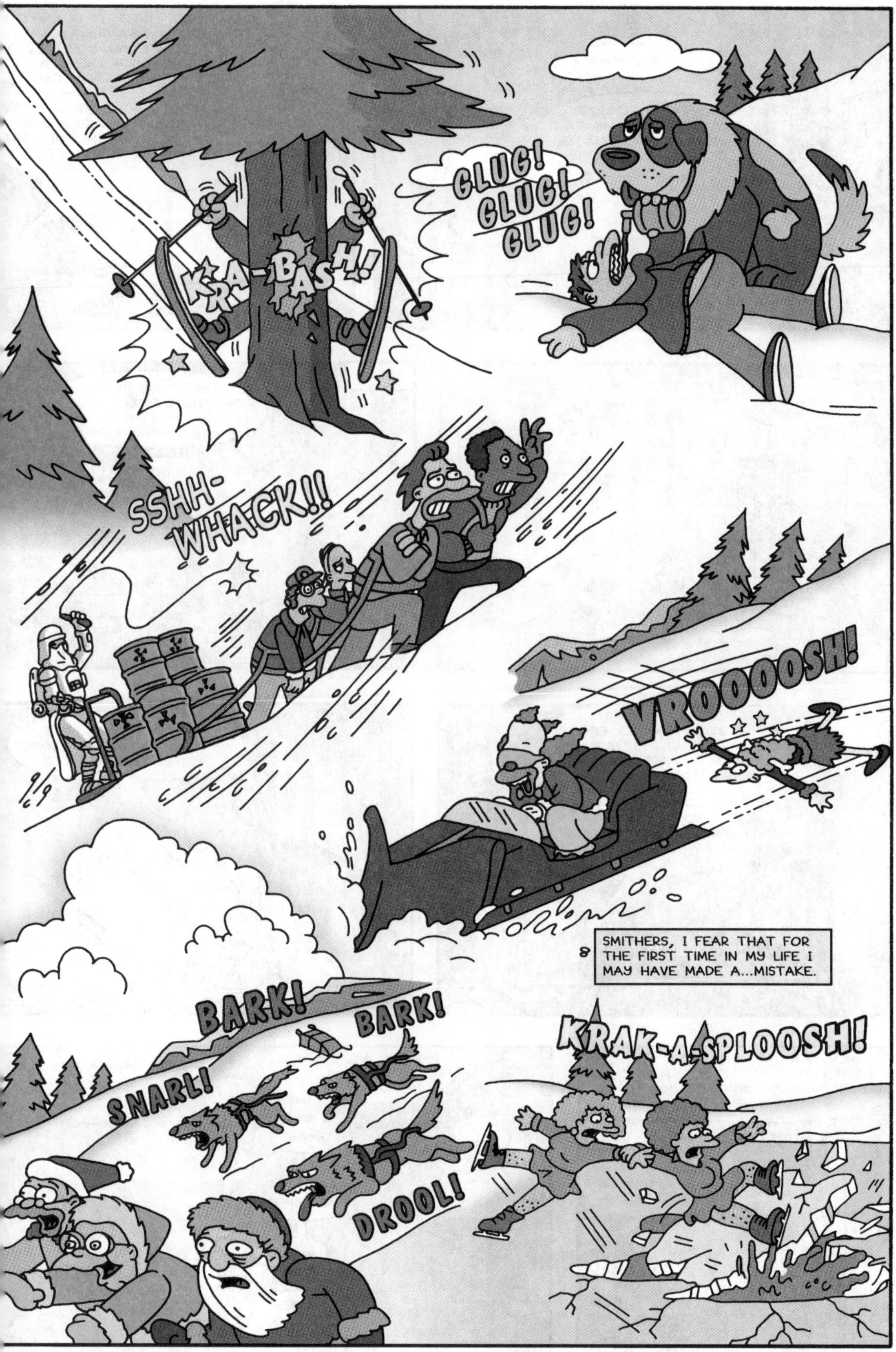
KRA-BASH!
GLUG! GLUG! GLUG!
SSHH-WHACK!!
VROOOOOSH!
SMITHERS, I FEAR THAT FOR THE FIRST TIME IN MY LIFE I MAY HAVE MADE A...MISTAKE.
BARK!
BARK!
SNARL!
DROOL!
KRAK-A-SPLOOSH!

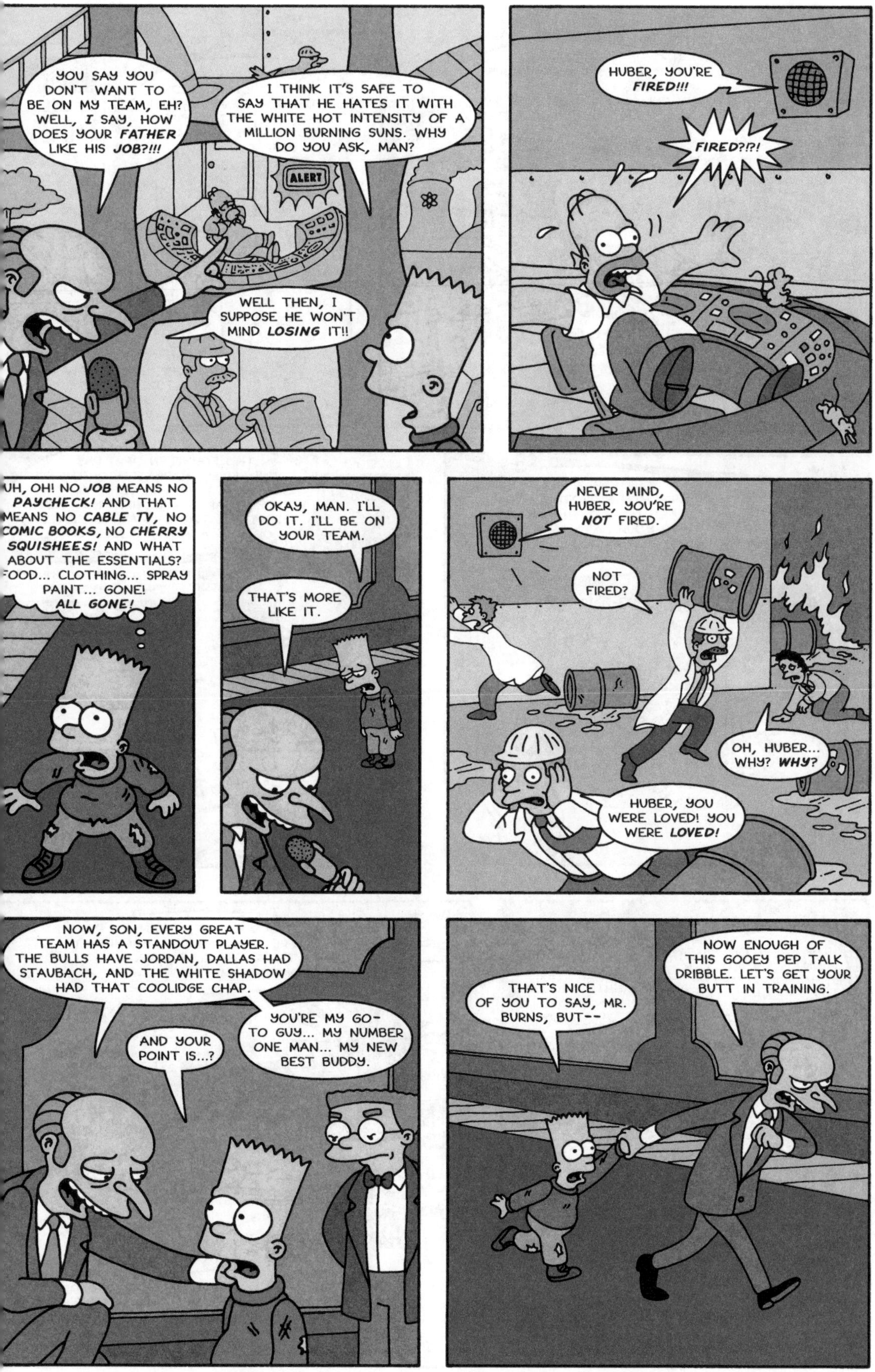

YOU SAY YOU DON'T WANT TO BE ON MY TEAM, EH? WELL, *I* SAY, HOW DOES YOUR ***FATHER*** LIKE HIS ***JOB?!!!***
I THINK IT'S SAFE TO SAY THAT HE HATES IT WITH THE WHITE HOT INTENSITY OF A MILLION BURNING SUNS. WHY DO YOU ASK, MAN?
ALERT
WELL THEN, I SUPPOSE HE WON'T MIND ***LOSING*** IT!!
HUBER, YOU'RE ***FIRED!!!***
FIRED?!?!
UH, OH! NO ***JOB*** MEANS NO ***PAYCHECK!*** AND THAT MEANS NO ***CABLE TV,*** NO ***COMIC BOOKS,*** NO ***CHERRY SQUISHEES!*** AND WHAT ABOUT THE ESSENTIALS? FOOD... CLOTHING... SPRAY PAINT... GONE! ***ALL GONE!***
OKAY, MAN. I'LL DO IT. I'LL BE ON YOUR TEAM.
THAT'S MORE LIKE IT.
NEVER MIND, HUBER, YOU'RE ***NOT*** FIRED.
NOT FIRED?
OH, HUBER... WHY? ***WHY?***
HUBER, YOU WERE LOVED! YOU WERE ***LOVED!***
NOW, SON, EVERY GREAT TEAM HAS A STANDOUT PLAYER. THE BULLS HAVE JORDAN, DALLAS HAD STAUBACH, AND THE WHITE SHADOW HAD THAT COOLIDGE CHAP.
AND YOUR POINT IS...?
YOU'RE MY GO-TO GUY... MY NUMBER ONE MAN... MY NEW BEST BUDDY.
THAT'S NICE OF YOU TO SAY, MR. BURNS, BUT--
NOW ENOUGH OF THIS GOOEY PEP TALK DRIBBLE. LET'S GET YOUR BUTT IN TRAINING.

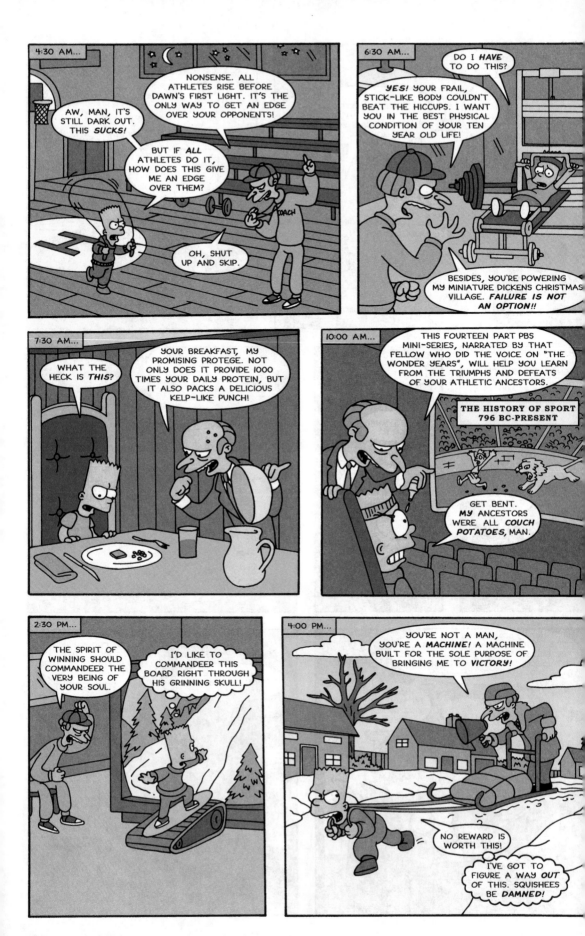

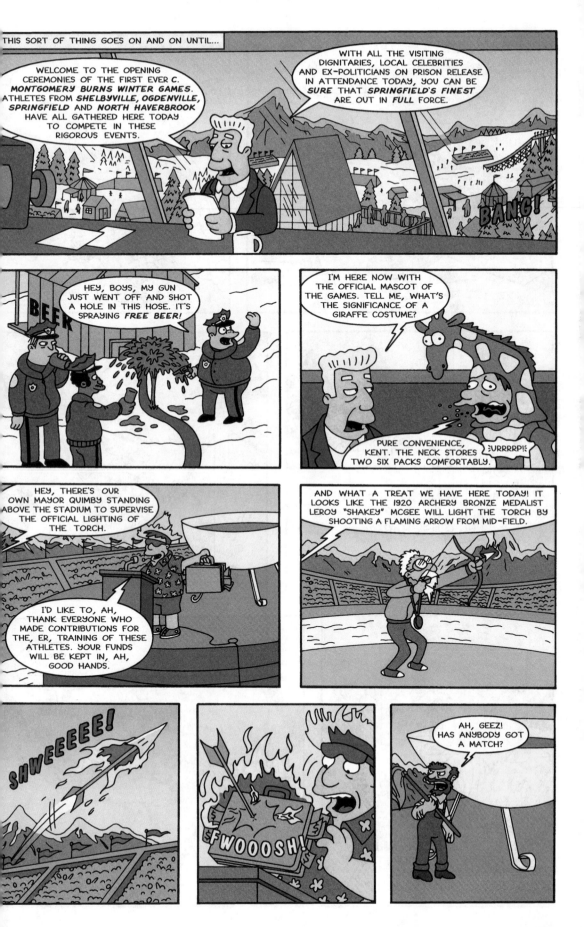

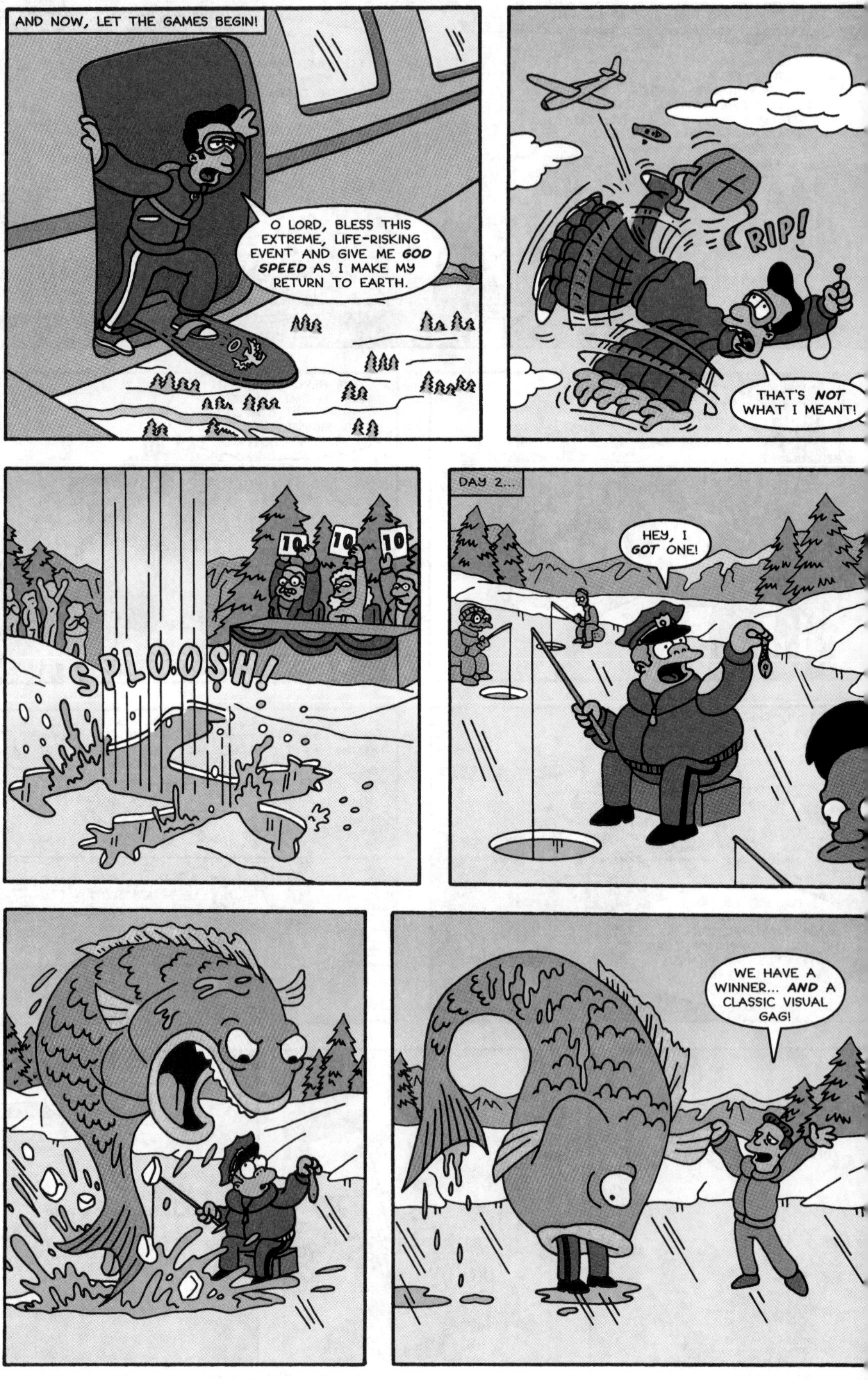
AND NOW, LET THE GAMES BEGIN!
O LORD, BLESS THIS EXTREME, LIFE-RISKING EVENT AND GIVE ME GOD SPEED AS I MAKE MY RETURN TO EARTH.
RIP!
THAT'S NOT WHAT I MEANT!
10 10 10
SPLOOSH!
DAY 2...
HEY, I GOT ONE!
WE HAVE A WINNER... AND A CLASSIC VISUAL GAG!

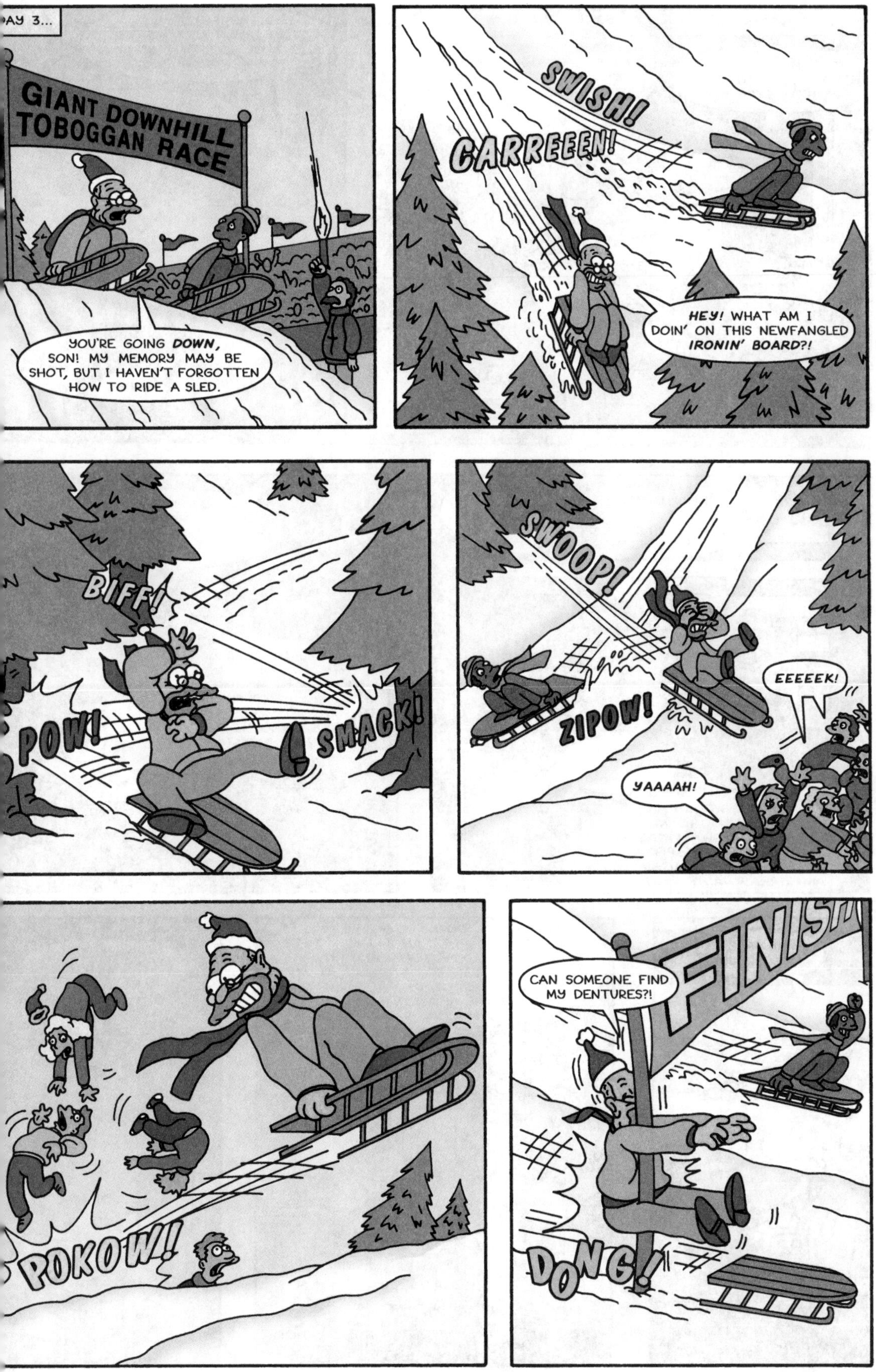
DAY 3...
GIANT DOWNHILL TOBOGGAN RACE
YOU'RE GOING DOWN, SON! MY MEMORY MAY BE SHOT, BUT I HAVEN'T FORGOTTEN HOW TO RIDE A SLED.
SWISH!
CARREEEN!
HEY! WHAT AM I DOIN' ON THIS NEWFANGLED IRONIN' BOARD?!
BIFF!
POW!
SMACK!
SWOOP!
ZIPOW!
EEEEEK!
YAAAAH!
POKOW!
FINISH
CAN SOMEONE FIND MY DENTURES?!
DONG!

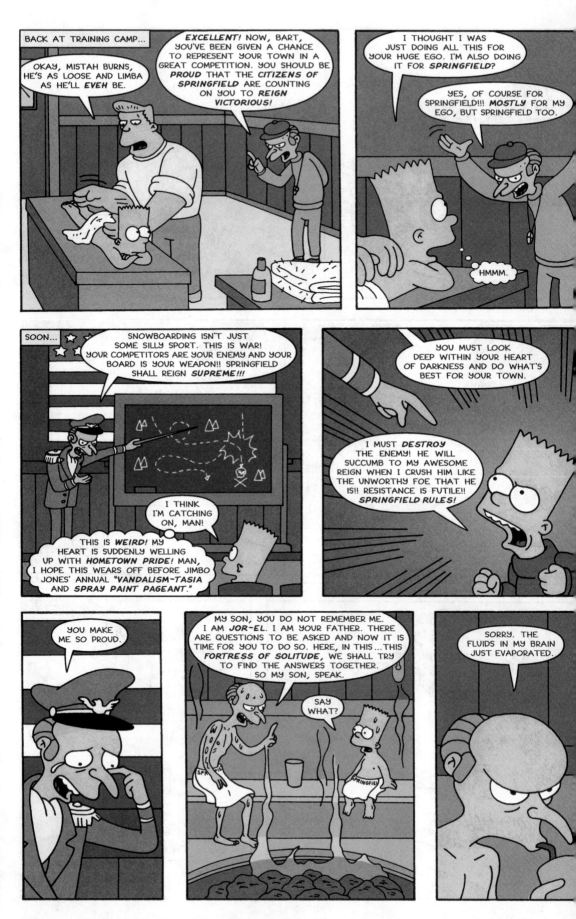

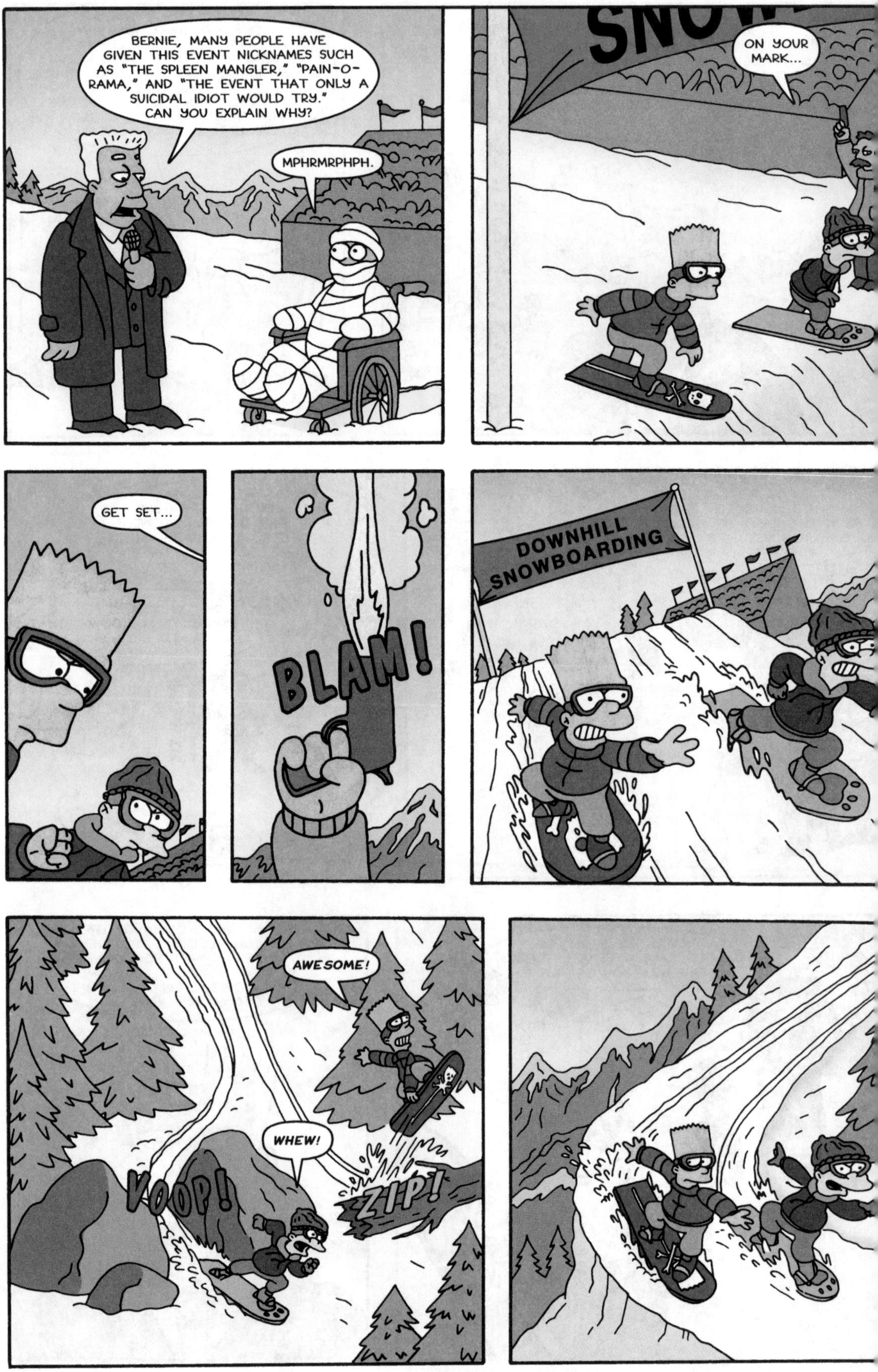
BERNIE, MANY PEOPLE HAVE GIVEN THIS EVENT NICKNAMES SUCH AS "THE SPLEEN MANGLER," "PAIN-O-RAMA," AND "THE EVENT THAT ONLY A SUICIDAL IDIOT WOULD TRY." CAN YOU EXPLAIN WHY?
MPHRMRPHPH.
SNOW
ON YOUR MARK...
GET SET...
BLAM!
DOWNHILL SNOWBOARDING
AWESOME!
WHEW!
VOOP!
ZIP!

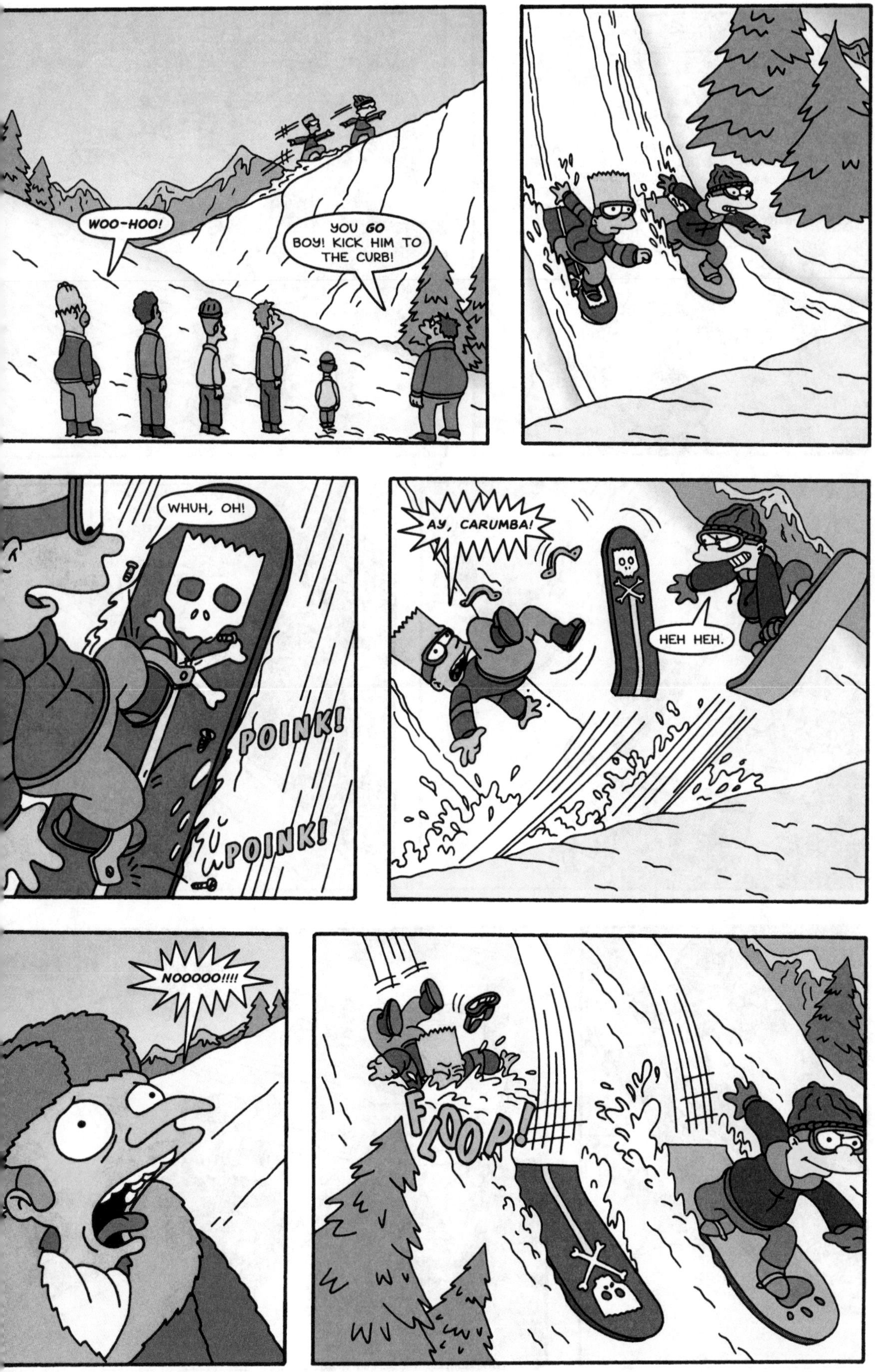
WOO-HOO!
YOU GO BOY! KICK HIM TO THE CURB!
WHUH, OH!
POINK!
POINK!
AY, CARUMBA!
HEH HEH.
NOOOOO!!!!
FLOOP!

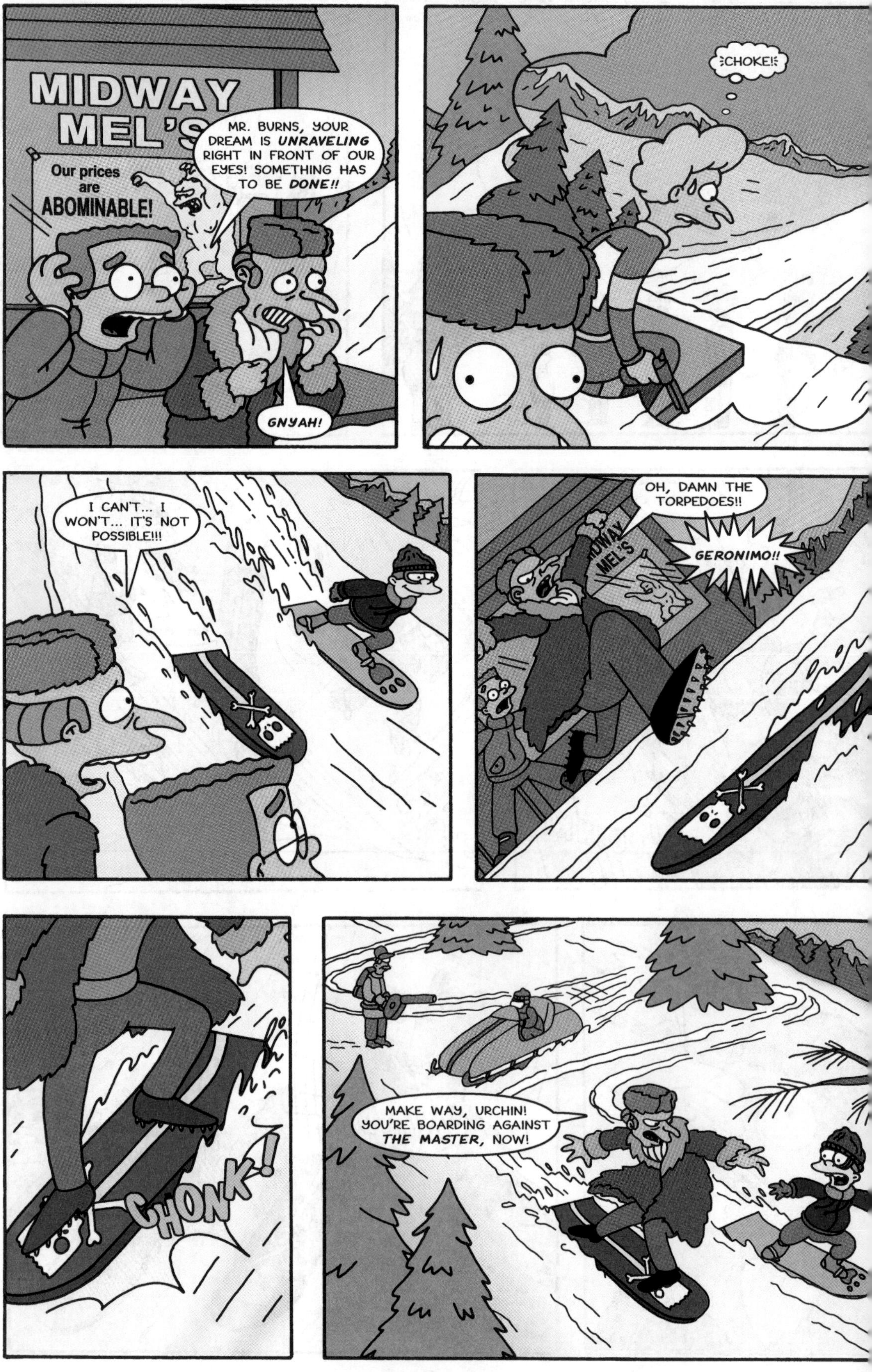
MIDWAY MEL'S
Our prices are ABOMINABLE!
MR. BURNS, YOUR DREAM IS UNRAVELING RIGHT IN FRONT OF OUR EYES! SOMETHING HAS TO BE DONE!!
GNYAH!
CHOKE!
I CAN'T... I WON'T... IT'S NOT POSSIBLE!!!
OH, DAMN THE TORPEDOES!!
GERONIMO!!
MEL'S
CHONK!
MAKE WAY, URCHIN! YOU'RE BOARDING AGAINST THE MASTER, NOW!

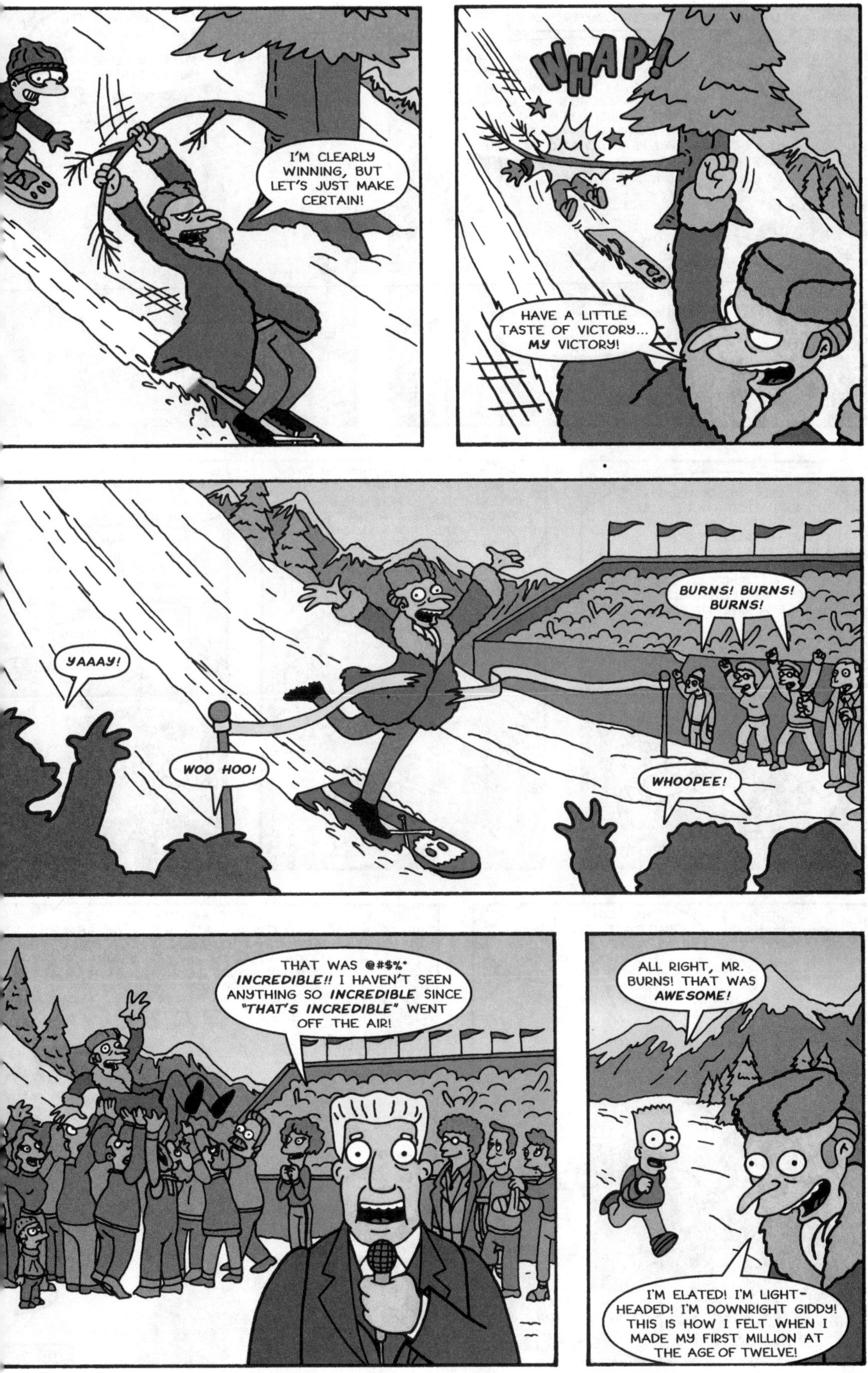
I'M CLEARLY WINNING, BUT LET'S JUST MAKE CERTAIN!
WHAP!
HAVE A LITTLE TASTE OF VICTORY... MY VICTORY!
BURNS! BURNS! BURNS!
YAAAY!
WOO HOO!
WHOOPEE!
THAT WAS @#$%* INCREDIBLE!! I HAVEN'T SEEN ANYTHING SO INCREDIBLE SINCE "THAT'S INCREDIBLE" WENT OFF THE AIR!
ALL RIGHT, MR. BURNS! THAT WAS AWESOME!
I'M ELATED! I'M LIGHT-HEADED! I'M DOWNRIGHT GIDDY! THIS IS HOW I FELT WHEN I MADE MY FIRST MILLION AT THE AGE OF TWELVE!

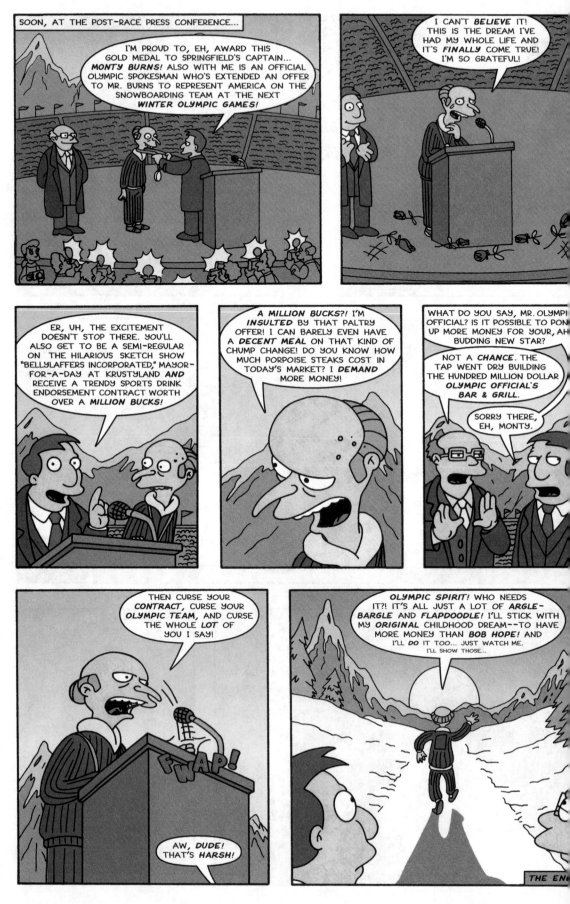

BELIEVE US, WE GET LETTERS! SO MANY, IN FACT, THAT WE HAVE LOST SIX INTERNS THIS YEAR ALONE TO MAIL-SLIDES AND OTHER BULK POSTAGE MISHAPS. DUE TO THIS INCREDIBLE (AND DANGEROUS) VOLUME OF MAIL, WE ARE UNABLE TO ANSWER YOUR LETTERS INDIVIDUALLY. BUT WE DO LISTEN TO YOUR IDEAS AND CRITICISMS, AS EVIDENCED IN THE FOLLOWING FEATURE! SEE YOUR DREAMS FOR BONGO COME TO LIFE IN THE NEXT FOUR PAGES AS WE TAKE A SIMPLE STORY AND PUT IT THROUGH...

THE SIMPSONS SUPPORTERS' SUGGESTION SPIN CYCLE!

FIRST, LET'S TAKE A LOOK AT WHAT OUR STORY WOULD LOOK LIKE WITHOUT YOUR VALUABLE INPUT. NEXT, SEE HOW YOUR LETTERS AFFECT BONGO'S UNIQUE BRAND OF STORYCRAFTING.

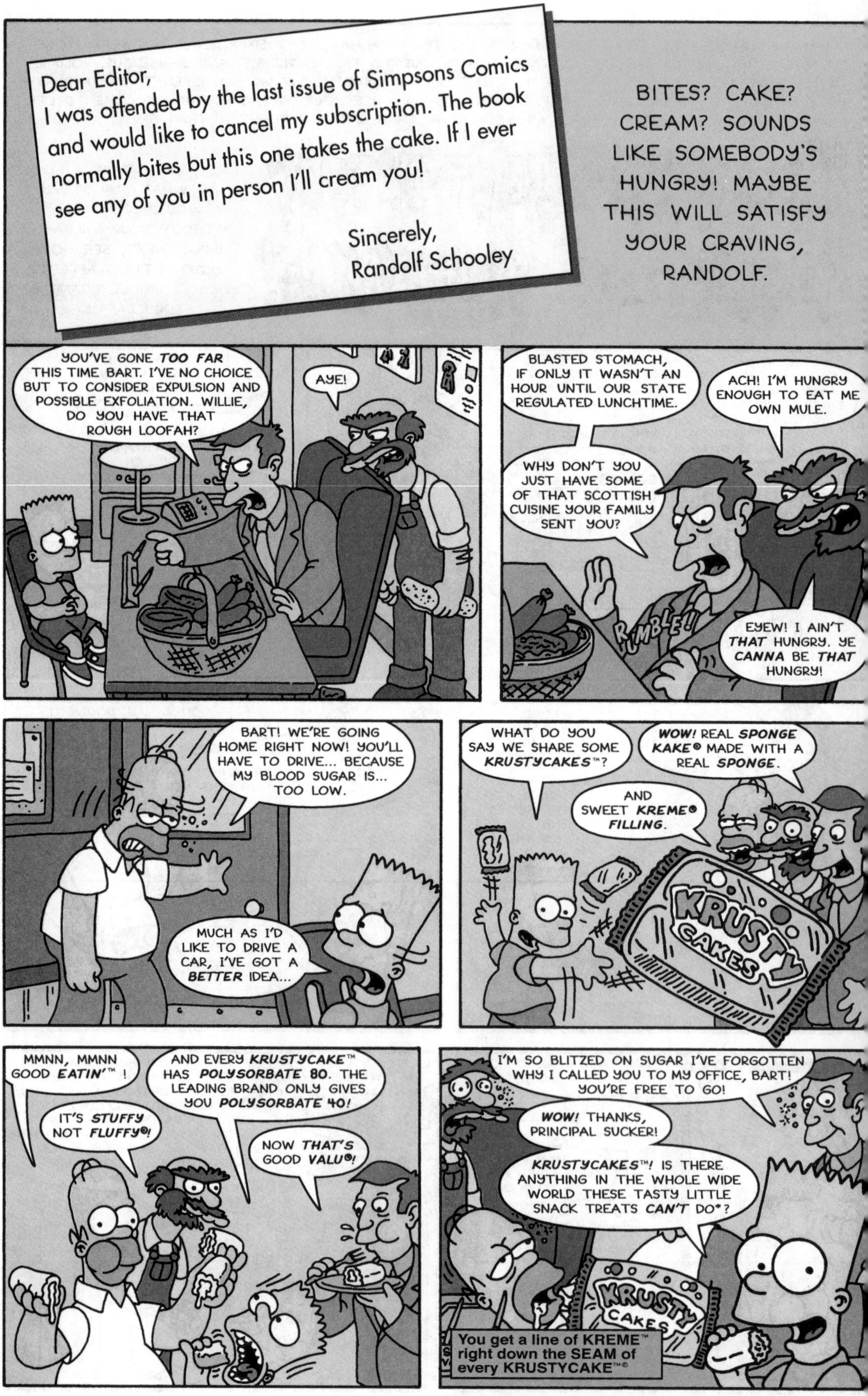

Dear Editor,
I was offended by the last issue of Simpsons Comics and would like to cancel my subscription. The book normally bites but this one takes the cake. If I ever see any of you in person I'll cream you!
Sincerely,
Randolf Schooley
BITES? CAKE? CREAM? SOUNDS LIKE SOMEBODY'S HUNGRY! MAYBE THIS WILL SATISFY YOUR CRAVING, RANDOLF.
YOU'VE GONE TOO FAR THIS TIME BART. I'VE NO CHOICE BUT TO CONSIDER EXPULSION AND POSSIBLE EXFOLIATION. WILLIE, DO YOU HAVE THAT ROUGH LOOFAH?
AYE!
BLASTED STOMACH, IF ONLY IT WASN'T AN HOUR UNTIL OUR STATE REGULATED LUNCHTIME.
ACH! I'M HUNGRY ENOUGH TO EAT ME OWN MULE.
WHY DON'T YOU JUST HAVE SOME OF THAT SCOTTISH CUISINE YOUR FAMILY SENT YOU?
RUMBLE!!
EYEW! I AIN'T THAT HUNGRY. YE CANNA BE THAT HUNGRY!
BART! WE'RE GOING HOME RIGHT NOW! YOU'LL HAVE TO DRIVE... BECAUSE MY BLOOD SUGAR IS... TOO LOW.
MUCH AS I'D LIKE TO DRIVE A CAR, I'VE GOT A BETTER IDEA...
WHAT DO YOU SAY WE SHARE SOME KRUSTYCAKES™?
WOW! REAL SPONGE KAKE® MADE WITH A REAL SPONGE.
AND SWEET KREME® FILLING.
KRUSTY CAKES
MMNN, MMNN GOOD EATIN'™ !
AND EVERY KRUSTYCAKE™ HAS POLYSORBATE 80. THE LEADING BRAND ONLY GIVES YOU POLYSORBATE 40!
IT'S STUFFY NOT FLUFFY®!
NOW THAT'S GOOD VALU®!
I'M SO BLITZED ON SUGAR I'VE FORGOTTEN WHY I CALLED YOU TO MY OFFICE, BART! YOU'RE FREE TO GO!
WOW! THANKS, PRINCIPAL SUCKER!
KRUSTYCAKES™! IS THERE ANYTHING IN THE WHOLE WIDE WORLD THESE TASTY LITTLE SNACK TREATS CAN'T DO*?
KRUSTY CAKES
You get a line of KREME™ right down the SEAM of every KRUSTYCAKE™©

*THIS IS A RHETORICAL QUESTION. PLEASE DO NOT SEND KRUSTY THE CLOWN OR HIS AGENTS ANY ANSWERS TO THIS QUESTION UNLESS ACCOMPANIED BY CHECKS OR MONEY ORDERS TO COVER LETTER DISPOSAL COSTS.

o the Editor,
Alternate timelines? Poetry contests? Amnesiacs dressed up as superheroes? Methinks your comics are getting a bit too highbrow for the kids. As our little ones are our most precious resource, couldn't you tell more children-oriented stories in your comics? Maybe a tale of happy anthropomorphic dinosaurs who juggle fruit or something?

Sincerely,
Ms. Susan M. Ferguson

MS. FERGUSON, WE TOO BELIEVE THAT CHILDREN ARE OUR FUTURE (THE GOOD FUTURE, NOT THE BAD ONE WHERE THE ROBOTS HUNT US DOWN FOR OUR SKIN). WITH THAT IN MIND, HERE'S ONE FOR THE KIDS...

Dear Editors,
Attention Deficit Disorder is a serious problem that...um...say, you know, if the French word for grape is raisin, what do they call raisins?

Catherine Kinsey

CATHERINE, WE UNDERSTAND YOUR PROBLEM AND SYMPATHIZE COMPLETELY. MANY OF US HERE AT **BONGO** SUFFER FROM SIMILAR MALADIES, SUCH AS "CHANNEL SURFER SYNDROME," "DOWNLOAD PATIENCE INADEQUACY," AND "MICROWAVE TIMER HYPOPLASIA." THIS ONE'S FOR YOU, CATHERINE. IT WON'T TAKE BUT A MINUTE.

ACH! THERE'S MORE MEAT IN ME *BOOT* THAN THIS *WEE BURGER.*

WELL BART, I WAS CERTAINLY UPSET AT YOU A FEW MINUTES AGO.

BUT I PROMISED TO TAKE CARE OF THINGS IN A THREATENING MANNER.

RIGHT.

EXCEPT FOR THE PART WHERE YOU ASKED SKINNER AND WILLIE TO COME *WITH* US TO KRUSTYBURGER. AND THEN TOLD THEM BOTH OUR PLAN JUST NOW.

AND WE FOOLED YOU *COMPLETELY!* WHAT A COUPLE OF FIRST CLASS *SUCKERS!* IT WAS A PERFECT PLAN!

D'OH!

SCRIPT: IAN BOOTHBY
PENCILS: PHIL ORTIZ
INKS: TIM BAVINGTON
LETTERS: JEANNINE BLACK
COLORS: NATHAN KANE
SURVEY SAYS: MATT GROENING

THE LONG AND SHORT OF IT.

82

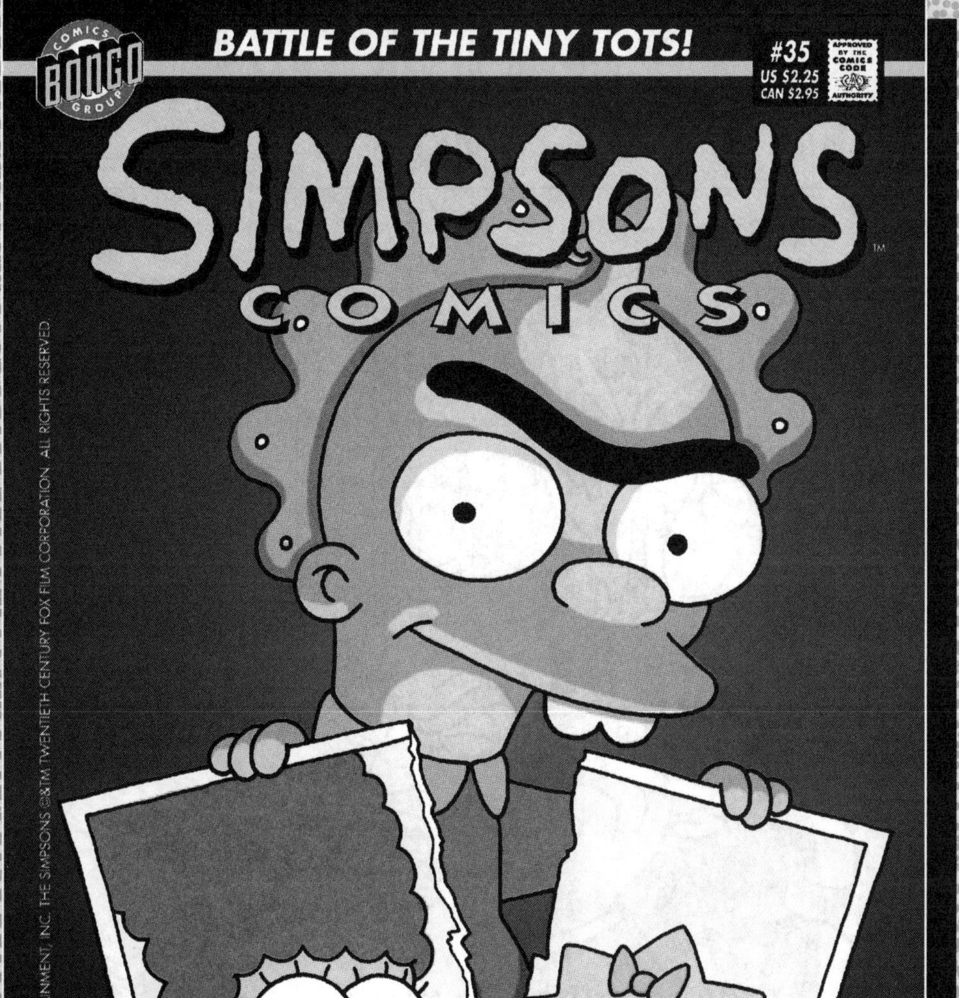

BONGO COMICS GROUP
BATTLE OF THE TINY TOTS!
#35
US $2.25
CAN $2.95
APPROVED BY THE COMICS CODE AUTHORITY
SIMPSONS
COMICS
©1998 BONGO ENTERTAINMENT, INC. THE SIMPSONS ©&TM TWENTIETH CENTURY FOX FILM CORPORATION. ALL RIGHTS RESERVED.
GROENING

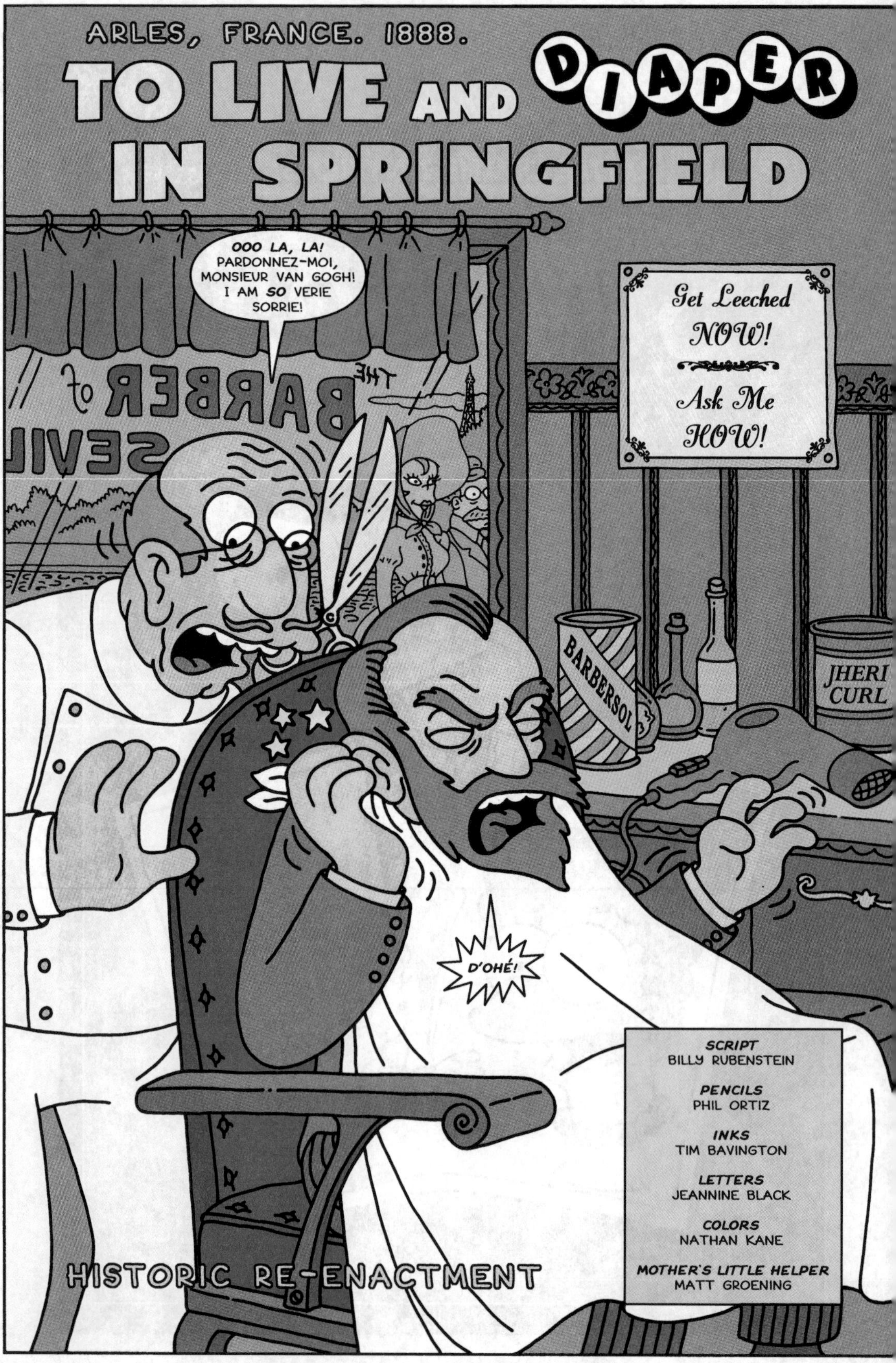
ARLES, FRANCE. 1888.
TO LIVE AND DIAPER IN SPRINGFIELD
OOO LA, LA! PARDONNEZ-MOI, MONSIEUR VAN GOGH! I AM SO VERIE SORRIE!
THE BARBER of SEVIL
Get Leeched NOW! Ask Me HOW!
BARBERSOL
JHERI CURL
D'OHÉ!
HISTORIC RE-ENACTMENT
SCRIPT
BILLY RUBENSTEIN
PENCILS
PHIL ORTIZ
INKS
TIM BAVINGTON
LETTERS
JEANNINE BLACK
COLORS
NATHAN KANE
MOTHER'S LITTLE HELPER
MATT GROENING

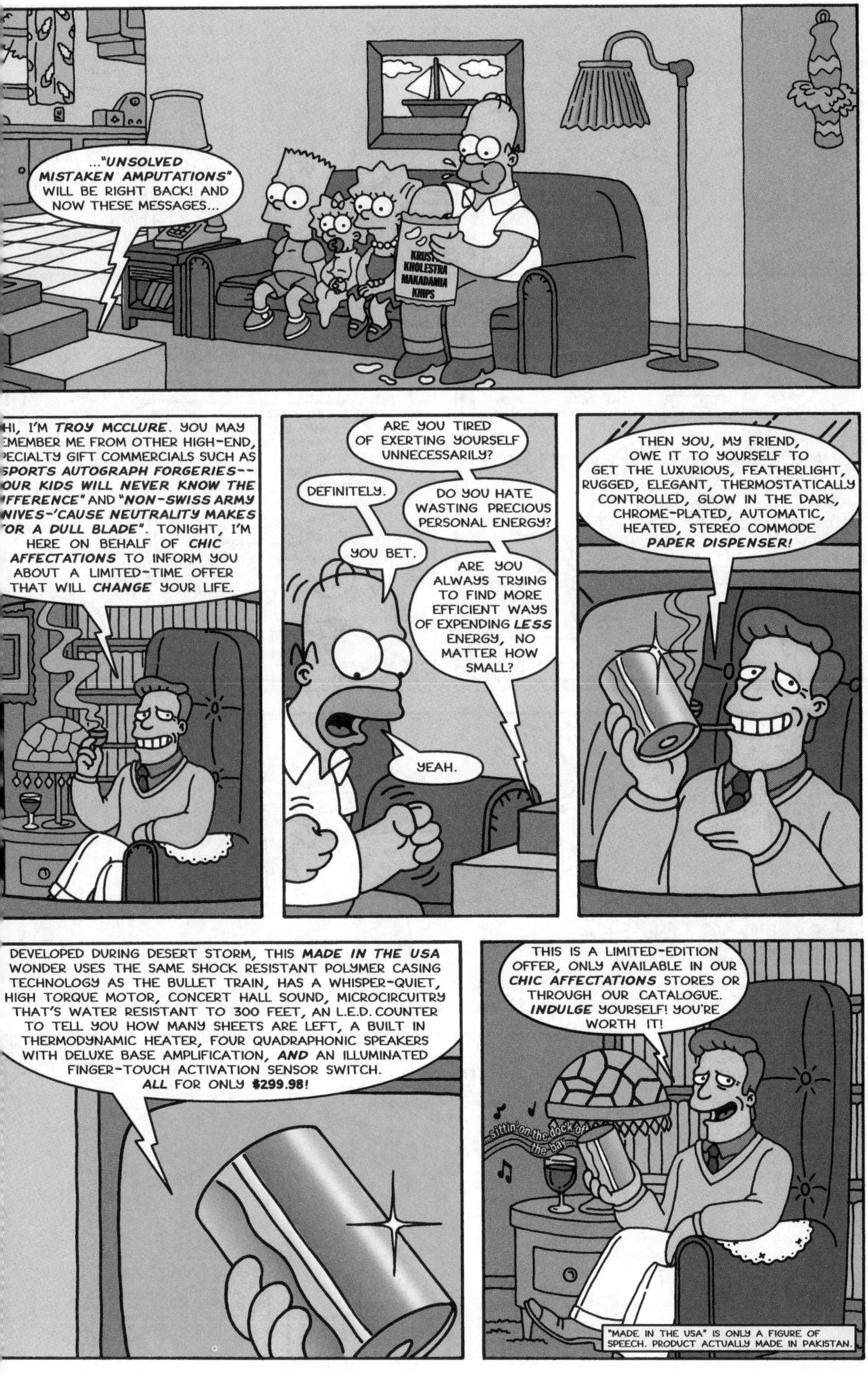

..."UNSOLVED MISTAKEN AMPUTATIONS" WILL BE RIGHT BACK! AND NOW THESE MESSAGES...
KRUSTY KHOLESTRA MAKADAMIA KHIPS
HI, I'M TROY MCCLURE. YOU MAY EMEMBER ME FROM OTHER HIGH-END, PECIALTY GIFT COMMERCIALS SUCH AS SPORTS AUTOGRAPH FORGERIES-- OUR KIDS WILL NEVER KNOW THE IFFERENCE" AND "NON-SWISS ARMY NIVES-'CAUSE NEUTRALITY MAKES OR A DULL BLADE". TONIGHT, I'M HERE ON BEHALF OF CHIC AFFECTATIONS TO INFORM YOU ABOUT A LIMITED-TIME OFFER THAT WILL CHANGE YOUR LIFE.
ARE YOU TIRED OF EXERTING YOURSELF UNNECESSARILY?
DEFINITELY.
DO YOU HATE WASTING PRECIOUS PERSONAL ENERGY?
YOU BET.
ARE YOU ALWAYS TRYING TO FIND MORE EFFICIENT WAYS OF EXPENDING LESS ENERGY, NO MATTER HOW SMALL?
YEAH.
THEN YOU, MY FRIEND, OWE IT TO YOURSELF TO GET THE LUXURIOUS, FEATHERLIGHT, RUGGED, ELEGANT, THERMOSTATICALLY CONTROLLED, GLOW IN THE DARK, CHROME-PLATED, AUTOMATIC, HEATED, STEREO COMMODE PAPER DISPENSER!
DEVELOPED DURING DESERT STORM, THIS MADE IN THE USA WONDER USES THE SAME SHOCK RESISTANT POLYMER CASING TECHNOLOGY AS THE BULLET TRAIN, HAS A WHISPER-QUIET, HIGH TORQUE MOTOR, CONCERT HALL SOUND, MICROCIRCUITRY THAT'S WATER RESISTANT TO 300 FEET, AN L.E.D. COUNTER TO TELL YOU HOW MANY SHEETS ARE LEFT, A BUILT IN THERMODYNAMIC HEATER, FOUR QUADRAPHONIC SPEAKERS WITH DELUXE BASE AMPLIFICATION, AND AN ILLUMINATED FINGER-TOUCH ACTIVATION SENSOR SWITCH. ALL FOR ONLY $299.98!
THIS IS A LIMITED-EDITION OFFER, ONLY AVAILABLE IN OUR CHIC AFFECTATIONS STORES OR THROUGH OUR CATALOGUE. INDULGE YOURSELF! YOU'RE WORTH IT!
...sittin' on the dock of the bay...
"MADE IN THE USA" IS ONLY A FIGURE OF SPEECH. PRODUCT ACTUALLY MADE IN PAKISTAN.

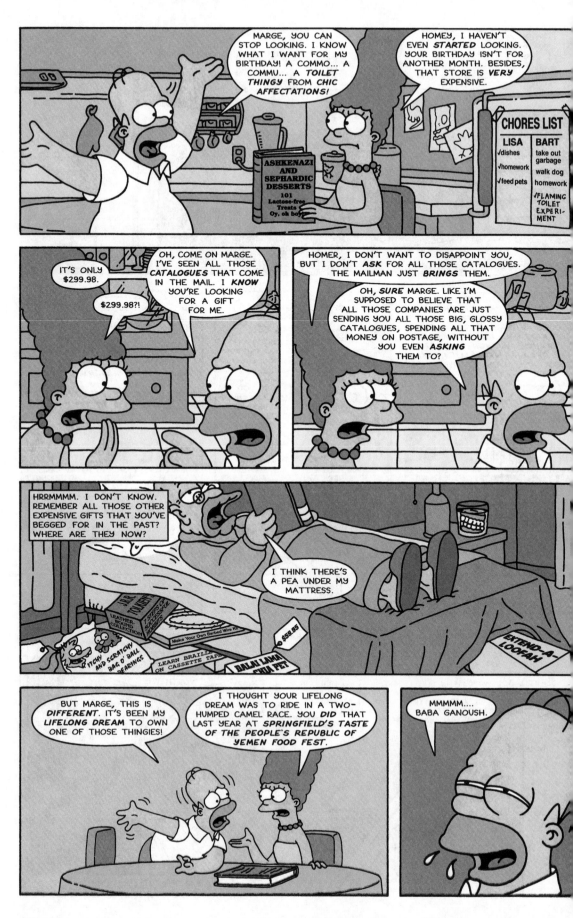

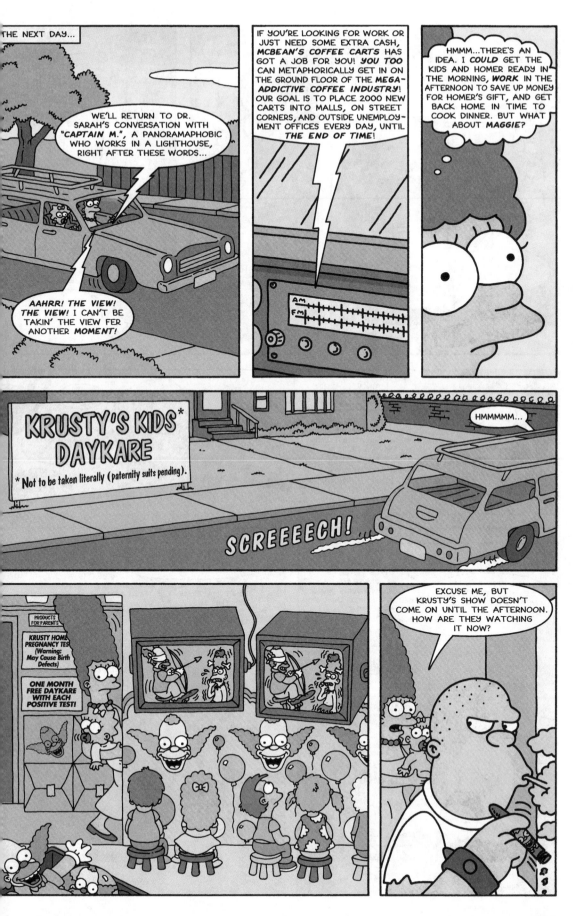

THE NEXT DAY...

WE'LL RETURN TO DR. SARAH'S CONVERSATION WITH "*CAPTAIN M.*", A PANORAMAPHOBIC WHO WORKS IN A LIGHTHOUSE, RIGHT AFTER THESE WORDS...

AAHRR! *THE VIEW! THE VIEW!* I CAN'T BE TAKIN' THE VIEW FER ANOTHER *MOMENT!*

IF YOU'RE LOOKING FOR WORK OR JUST NEED SOME EXTRA CASH, *MCBEAN'S COFFEE CARTS* HAS GOT A JOB FOR YOU! *YOU TOO* CAN METAPHORICALLY GET IN ON THE GROUND FLOOR OF THE *MEGA-ADDICTIVE COFFEE INDUSTRY*! OUR GOAL IS TO PLACE 2000 NEW CARTS INTO MALLS, ON STREET CORNERS, AND OUTSIDE UNEMPLOYMENT OFFICES EVERY DAY, UNTIL *THE END OF TIME!*

HMMM...THERE'S AN IDEA. I *COULD* GET THE KIDS AND HOMER READY IN THE MORNING, *WORK* IN THE AFTERNOON TO SAVE UP MONEY FOR HOMER'S GIFT, AND GET BACK HOME IN TIME TO COOK DINNER. BUT WHAT ABOUT *MAGGIE?*

KRUSTY'S KIDS* DAYKARE

* Not to be taken literally (paternity suits pending).

HMMMMM...

SCREEEECH!

PRODUCTS FOR PARENTS

KRUSTY HOME PREGNANCY TEST (Warning: May Cause Birth Defects)

ONE MONTH FREE DAYKARE WITH EACH POSITIVE TEST!

EXCUSE ME, BUT KRUSTY'S SHOW DOESN'T COME ON UNTIL THE AFTERNOON. HOW ARE THEY WATCHING IT NOW?

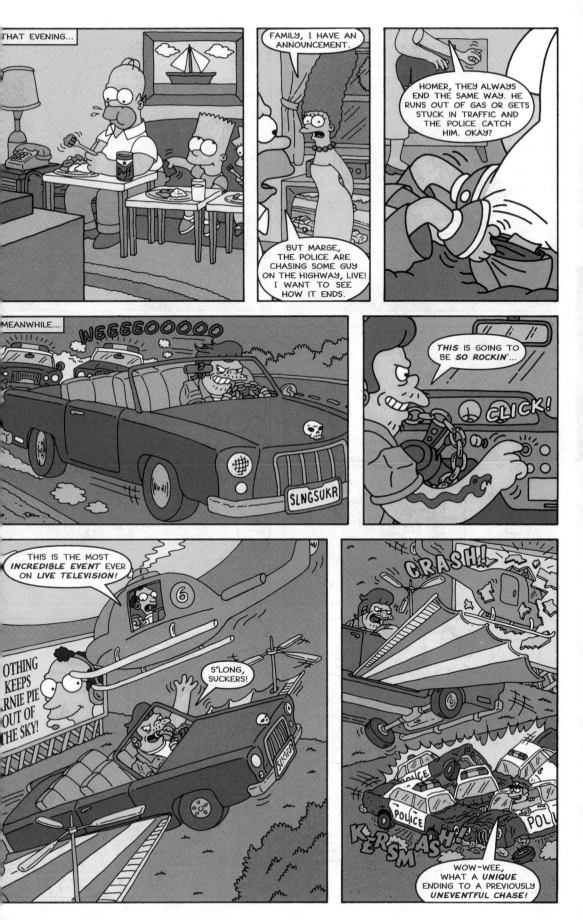

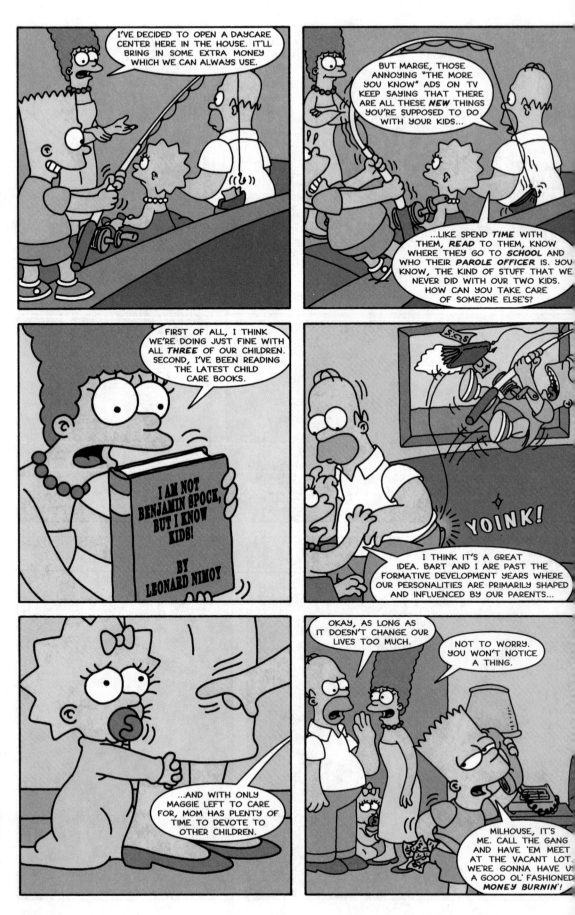

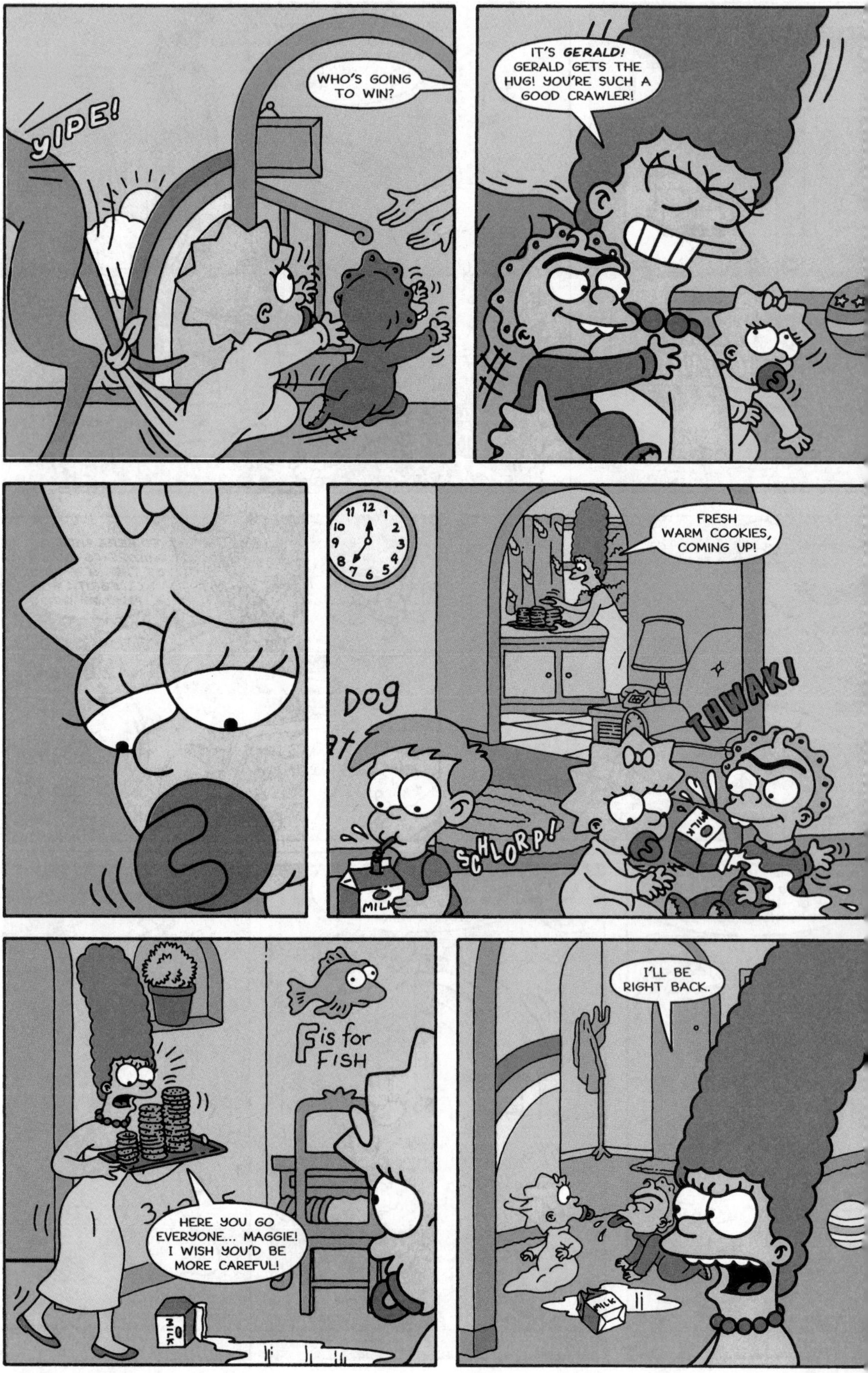
YIPE!
WHO'S GOING TO WIN?
IT'S GERALD! GERALD GETS THE HUG! YOU'RE SUCH A GOOD CRAWLER!
FRESH WARM COOKIES, COMING UP!
DOG
THWAK!
SCHLORP!
MILK
MILK
F is for FISH
HERE YOU GO EVERYONE... MAGGIE! I WISH YOU'D BE MORE CAREFUL!
MILK
I'LL BE RIGHT BACK.
MILK

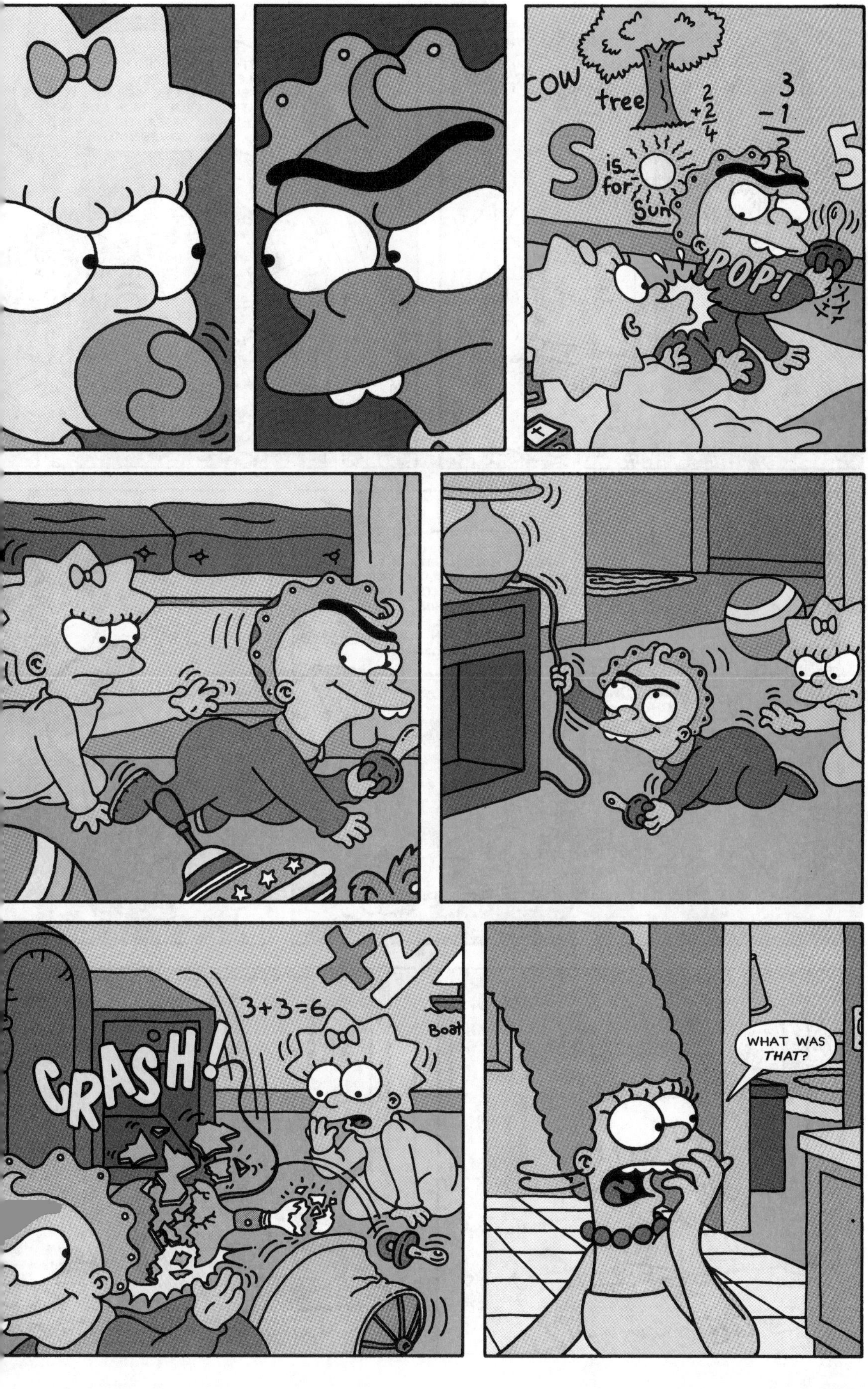

COW
tree
2
+2
4
3
-1
2
S
is
for
Sun
5
POP!
3+3=6
Boat
CRASH!
WHAT WAS THAT?

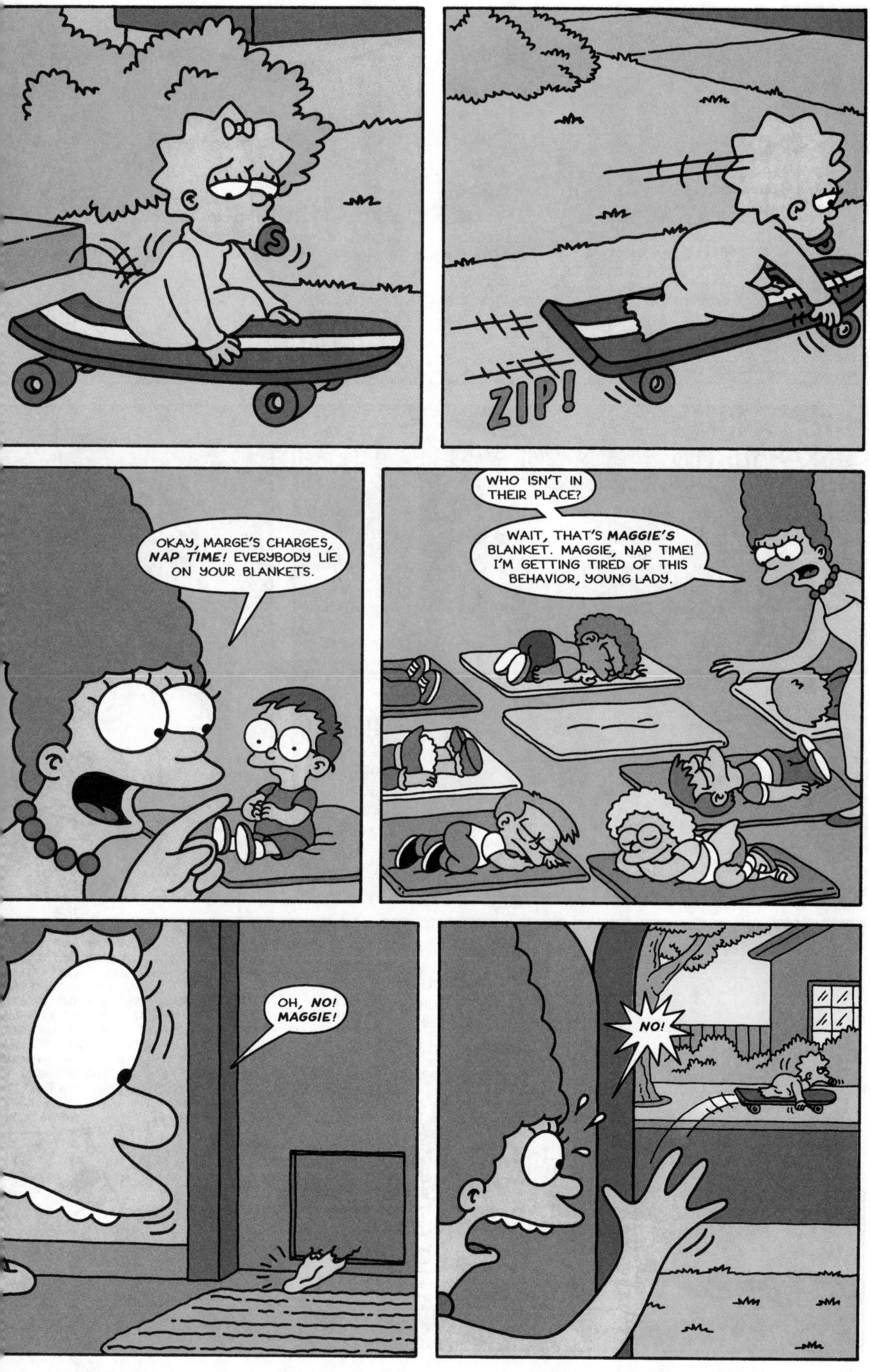
ZIP!
OKAY, MARGE'S CHARGES, *NAP TIME!* EVERYBODY LIE ON YOUR BLANKETS.
WHO ISN'T IN THEIR PLACE?
WAIT, THAT'S *MAGGIE'S* BLANKET. MAGGIE, NAP TIME! I'M GETTING TIRED OF THIS BEHAVIOR, YOUNG LADY.
OH, *NO!* *MAGGIE!*
NO!

101

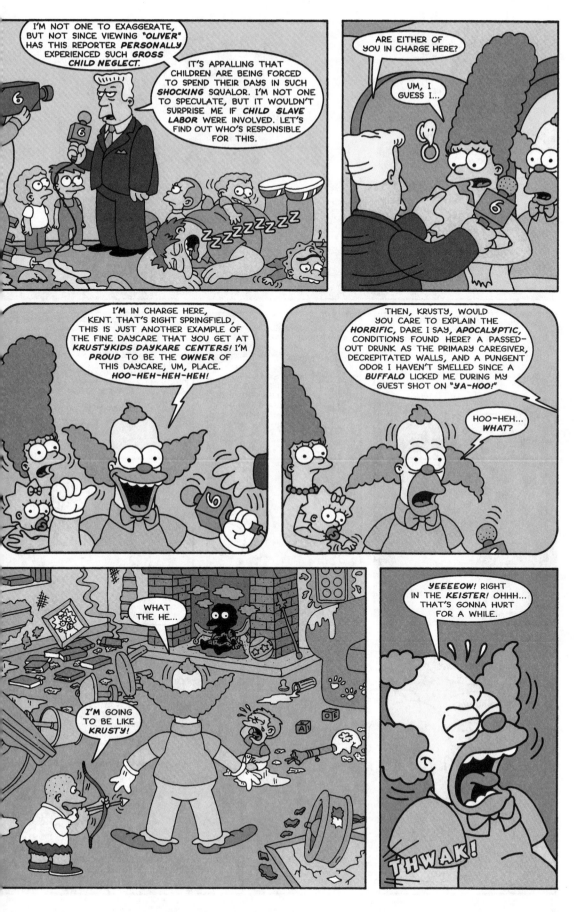

103

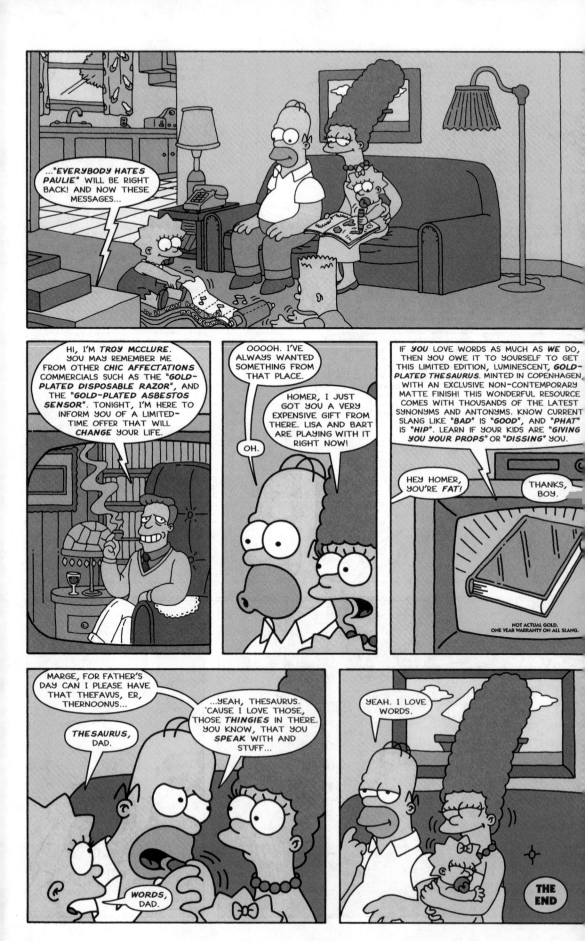

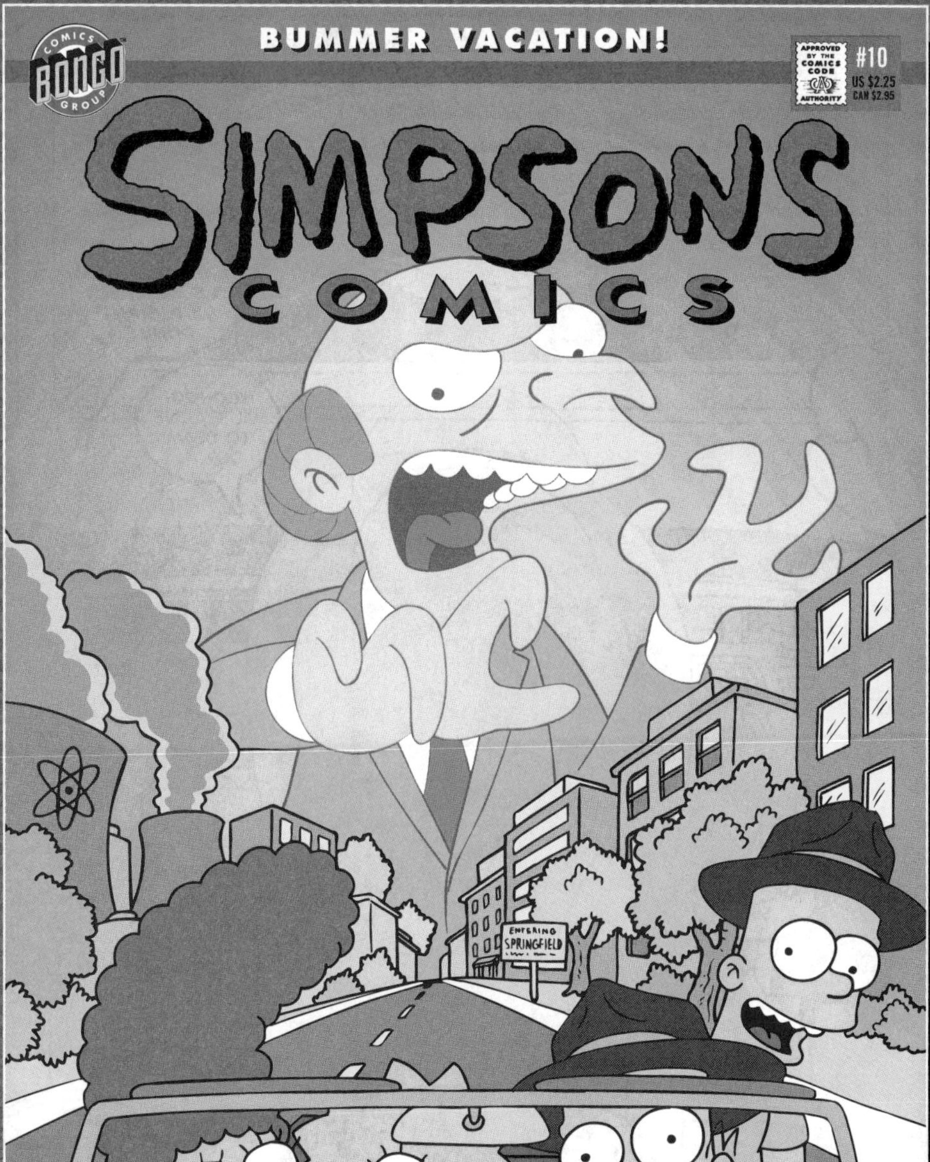
BUMMER VACATION!
#10
US $2.25
CAN $2.95
APPROVED BY THE COMICS CODE AUTHORITY
SIMPSONS
COMICS
ENTERING SPRINGFIELD
© 1995 BONGO ENTERTAINMENT, INC. THE SIMPSONS © & TM TWENTIETH CENTURY FOX FILM CORPORATION. ALL RIGHTS RESERVED.

FAN-TASTY ISLAND

WRITING
JEFF
ROSENTHAL

LAYOUTS
LUIS
ESCOBAR

PENCILS
TIM
BAVINGTON

INKS
TIM BAVINGTON, BILL MORRISON,
ROBERT KRAMER & DAVID MOWRY

COLOR
NATHAN & ELECTRIC
KANE   CRAYON

LETTERING
RICHARD STARKINGS
AND COMICRAFT

TOUR GUIDE
MATT
GROENING

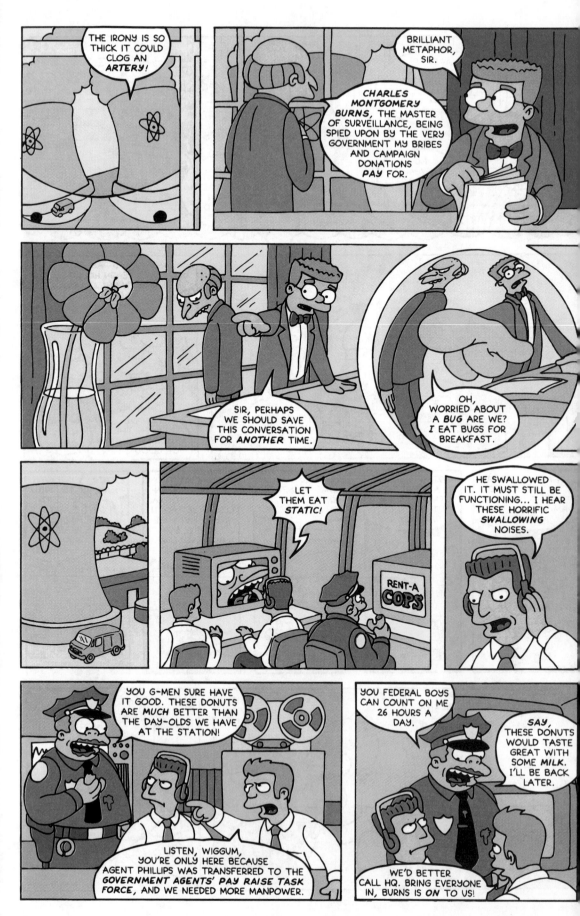

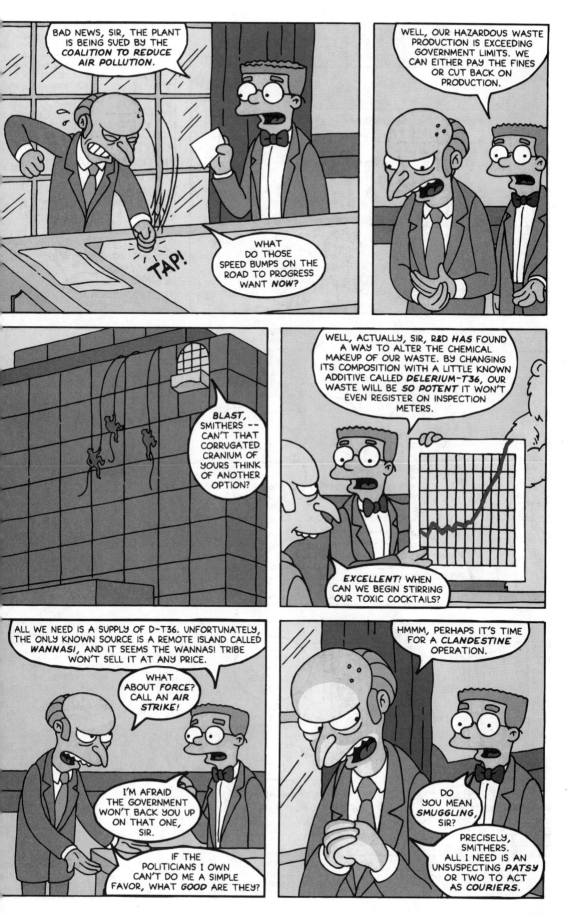

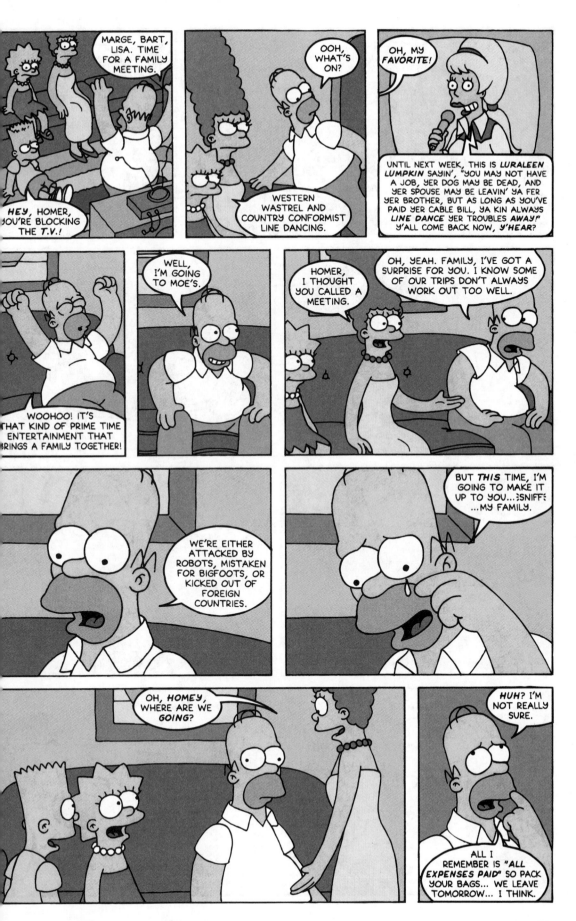

120

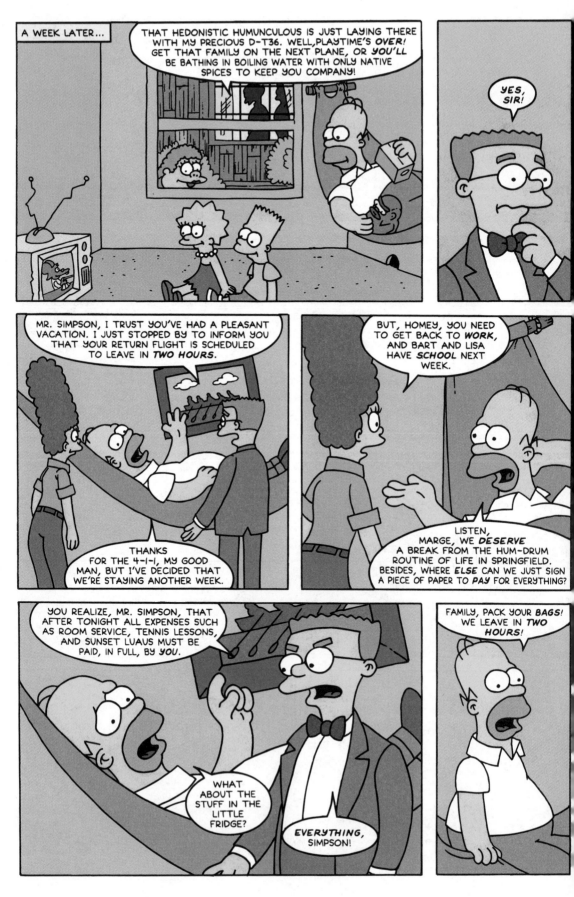

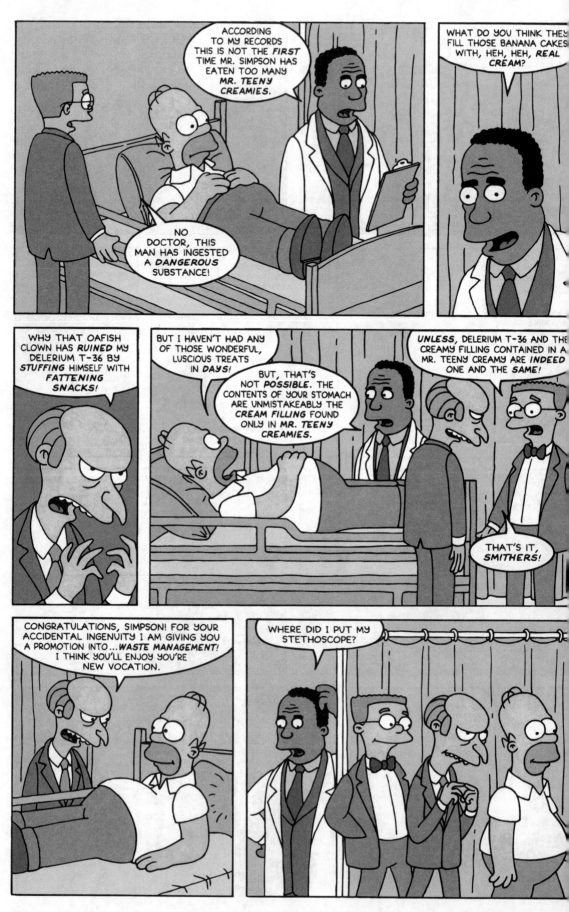